11+ English

For GL Assessment

It's no secret that the GL 11+ test can be seriously tricky. But don't worry — this CGP Practice Book will give children a brilliant headstart on their test preparation.

In the first few sections, they can practise answering questions on one topic at a time. Then, when they're ready for more realistic 11+ practice, give the Assessment Tests a try.

It's all set at just the right level for ages 8-9, so it's perfect for building their confidence. And with detailed answers included at the back of the book, marking is a breeze!

How to access your free Online Edition

This book includes a free Online Edition to read on your PC, Mac or tablet.
You'll just need to go to cgpbooks.co.uk/extras and enter this code:

0339 2014 0351 7917

By the way, this code only works for one person. If somebody else has used this book before you, they might have already claimed the Online Edition.

Practice Book — Ages 8-9
with Assessment Tests

How to use this Practice Book

This book is divided into two parts — themed question practice and assessment tests. There are answers and detailed explanations at the back of the book.

Themed question practice

- Each page contains practice questions divided by topic. Use these pages to work out your child's strengths and the areas they find tricky. The questions get harder down each page.

- Your child can use the smiley face tick boxes to evaluate how confident they feel with each topic.

Assessment tests

- The second half of the book contains eight assessment tests, each with a comprehension text and a matching set of questions, as well as a set of questions on grammar, spelling and punctuation. They take a similar form to the real test.

- You can print multiple-choice answer sheets so your child can practise the tests as if they're sitting the real thing — visit cgpbooks.co.uk/11plus/answer-sheets or scan the QR code.

- Use the printable answer sheets if you want your child to do each test more than once.

- If you want to give your child timed practice, give them a time limit of 30 minutes for each test, and ask them to work as quickly and carefully as they can.

- The tests get harder from 1-8, so don't be surprised if your child finds the later ones more tricky.

- Your child should aim for a mark of around 85% (26 questions correct) in each test. If they score less than this, use their results to work out the areas they need more practice on.

- If they haven't managed to finish the test in time, they need to work on increasing their speed, whereas if they have made a lot of mistakes, they need to work more carefully.

- Keep track of your child's scores using the progress chart at the end of the book.

Published by CGP

Editors:
Emma Elder, Heather Gregson, Holly Poynton, Jo Sharrock, Camilla Simson

Contributors:
Chloe Buckley, Steve Martin, Julie Moxon, Lucy Towle, Paul Warnes

With thanks to Joe Brazier, Jennifer Underwood and Janet Berkeley for the proofreading.

With thanks to Jane Ellingham for the copyright research.

Please note that CGP is not associated with GL Assessment in any way. This book does not include any official questions and is not endorsed by GL Assessment.

ISBN: 978 1 78908 153 4

Printed by Zenith Print & Packaging Ltd, Pontypridd.
Clipart from Corel®

Based on the classic CGP style created by Richard Parsons.
Text, design, layout and original illustrations © Coordination Group Publications Ltd. (CGP) 2018
All rights reserved.

Photocopying this book is not permitted, even if you have a CLA licence.
Extra copies are available from CGP with next day delivery • 0800 1712 712 • www.cgpbooks.co.uk

Contents

Section One — Grammar

Tick off the check box for each topic as you go along.

Parts of Speech .... 2 ✓
Verbs 4
Mixed Grammar Questions 6

Section Two — Punctuation

Starting and Ending Sentences 8
Commas 9
Apostrophes 10
Inverted Commas 12
Mixed Punctuation Questions 14

Section Three — Spelling

Plurals 16
Homophones 17
Prefixes and Suffixes 18
Awkward Spellings 19
Mixed Spelling Questions 20

Section Four — Writers' Techniques

Alliteration and Onomatopoeia 22
Imagery 23
Synonyms 24
Antonyms 25

Section Five — Writing

Creative Writing 26
Non-Fiction Writing 28

Assessment Tests

Test 1 30
Test 2 35
Test 3 40
Test 4 45
Test 5 50
Test 6 55
Test 7 60
Test 8 65

Glossary 70
Answers 71
Progress Chart 86

Section One — Grammar

Parts of Speech

Nouns & Pronouns

Underline the word in each sentence which matches the part of speech in brackets. For example:

I crept up to the hidden <u>door</u> and pulled it open. **(noun)**

1. My cat is extremely old and grumpy. **(noun)**

2. We think that Margot dances beautifully. **(noun)**

3. Caley hasn't told her the top-secret information. **(pronoun)**

4. The pack of wolves made Jo and her friends nervous. **(collective noun)**

5. A green-eyed monster swam slowly past us. **(noun)**

6. The tortoise in the flower bed is ours. **(pronoun)**

7. He really wants to eat at the new restaurant. **(pronoun)**

8. The river flowed past the flock of birds. **(collective noun)**

Hint: Remember, nouns are naming words.

/ 8

Nouns

Add your own words before and after the following nouns to create your own noun phrases. For example:

the cyclist   <u>the tired cyclist in the yellow jersey</u>

9. the bananas

_____

10. the police officer

_____

11. the lion

_____

Hint: Noun phrases are made up of a noun and any words that describe it.

/ 3

Parts of Speech

Adjectives & Adverbs

Underline the word in each sentence which matches the part of speech in brackets. For example:

The judge said that Calvin had a <u>fantastic</u> voice. **(adjective)**

1. Herbert was a famous explorer. **(adjective)**

2. We sprinted quickly past the old haunted house. **(adverb)**

3. A professional chef did a demonstration at school. **(adjective)**

4. Meredith had always wanted a funny clown at the party. **(adjective)**

5. I was trying desperately not to laugh during his speech. **(adverb)**

6. I listened to the teacher as she gave the important instructions. **(adjective)**

7. The bride walked confidently down the aisle of the church. **(adverb)**

/ 7

Adverbs

Underline the best adverb to complete each sentence. For example:

The baby yawned **(<u>sleepily</u> fiercely)** in its cot.

8. The men danced **(wisely gracefully)** across the stage.

9. Rivers often flow more **(kindly swiftly)** after heavy rain.

10. The fishermen sang **(instantly cheerfully)** all the way home.

11. Leopards are **(closely slowly)** related to lions.

12. The whole class **(obediently badly)** followed the teacher out of the door.

13. Sina marched **(boldly endlessly)** to the cave to face the dragon.

14. The chocolate sauce smelt **(consistently faintly)** of garlic.

/ 7

Verbs

Verbs — Underline the verb in each sentence. For example:

I <u>finished</u> my book at school.

1. Harry went to Nottingbury by bus.

2. Lyra loves baked beans with mashed potato.

3. We bought sandwiches from the supermarket.

4. Ashleigh danced from sunset to sunrise.

5. Briony took the last slice of pizza.

6. Alfred snored loudly during the school play.

7. After 8 o'clock, I shut the curtains in my bedroom.

/ 7

Verbs — Underline the correct verb from the brackets to complete each sentence. For example:

Kristin **(play played)** golf yesterday.

8. Ana **(sang sing)** beautifully in the concert.

9. Monty, our pet hamster, **(escaped escapes)** from his cage last night.

10. When I got home, I **(ate eat)** a delicious sandwich.

11. I **(want wanted)** to build a snowman because it is snowing.

12. Lucas **(kept keeps)** his P.E. kit in his locker until it went mouldy.

13. Geraint **(hung hang)** his coat on the peg by the door.

14. Michelle **(had have)** never been abroad before the exchange trip.

/ 7

Section One — Grammar

Verbs

Write the verb in brackets in the past tense. For example:

Mo (**give**) __gave__ Katie a birthday present.

1. Minna ran away from the dog that (**race**) _____ towards her.
2. Wen (**look**) _____ around the carriage for his dad.
3. Fin (**bring**) _____ his colouring pencils to the art class.
4. Henry (**take**) _____ the bus to work on Wednesday.
5. Paula had made a picnic which they (**eat**) _____ in the park.
6. Mary joined the knitting club and (**make**) _____ a scarf.
7. Gary (**think**) _____ that the Brussels sprouts tasted awful.

Hint: Some words are irregular and several letters may change when they change tense.

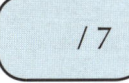

For each sentence, rewrite the verb in bold in the present tense so that the sentence still makes sense. For example:

I **picked** raspberries in the garden. ___pick___

8. Ibrahim **clapped** to celebrate the victory. _____
9. Mette **wished** that she could wear trousers to school. _____
10. The orange jelly **wobbled** gently on the tray. _____
11. Leon **chose** to join the orchestra. _____
12. Hannah **left** the building by the back staircase. _____
13. I **blew** a huge bubble in the bright sunlight. _____
14. Maria **bought** the tartan trousers. _____

Section One — Grammar

Mixed Grammar Questions

> Underline the word in each sentence which matches the part of speech in brackets. For example:
>
> <u>Kyle</u> couldn't believe what he saw. **(proper noun)**

1. When the orange ball rolled towards the river, Callum chased after it. **(adjective)**

2. The mouse stayed very still so that Mary wouldn't spot her. **(proper noun)**

3. When I left the caravan, I could hear someone talking loudly. **(adverb)**

4. The cat has completely ruined my favourite jumper. **(adjective)**

5. Lucia had been waiting patiently for fifteen minutes. **(adverb)**

/ 5

6. The bird landed on the branch without a sound. **(verb)**

7. Are you really going to run a marathon on Sunday? **(common noun)**

8. The picture on the wall by the window is mine. **(pronoun)**

9. The diamond ring sparkled in the sunlight. **(verb)**

10. Jill carried the frightened child safely through the stream. **(adjective)**

/ 5

11. Stu had already marked a spot for me to plant the roses. **(adverb)**

12. The policeman had to remind him of the speed limit. **(pronoun)**

13. One day, when I'm older, I want to own a farm. **(adjective)**

14. I was afraid to play the antique piano. **(common noun)**

15. The lantern blew out of my hands in the strong wind. **(verb)**

/ 5

Section One — Grammar

Mixed Grammar Questions

> Underline the correct word from the brackets to complete each sentence. For example:
>
> I **(sit <u>sat</u> sitting)** very still while he painted my portrait.

Hint: Read the sentence out loud to yourself to help you choose the correct word.

1. We **(works worked working)** really hard to win the dance competition.

2. The certificate **(tears tearing tore)** in half when they both grabbed it.

3. Milena was **(watching watch watches)** the TV when her brother arrived.

4. The nurse is **(careful caring careless)** for his patients.

5. Dad **(kind kindly kindness)** offered to drive us home after the party.

/ 5

6. Tola is going to meet **(your yours you)** at the bus station.

7. Gus **(throw threw throws)** the cricket ball the furthest at last year's sports day.

8. The **(bunch team flock)** of sheep was in the middle of the road.

9. The sun was **(shine shone shining)** through the gap in the blinds.

10. Henry's trip to France was **(him his its)** first holiday abroad.

/ 5

11. Ava showed great **(brave bravely bravery)** by rescuing the cat from the tree.

12. Nena had **(run ran runs)** around the park in the morning before work.

13. Geoff whistled **(soft softly softness)** as he cleaned the car.

14. My sister **(has have had)** brown hair before she dyed it purple.

15. Beth **(lights lit light)** the candles in the sitting room yesterday.

/ 5

Section One — Grammar

Section Two — Punctuation

Starting and Ending Sentences

Add a question mark (?) or an exclamation mark (!) to the end of each sentence. For example:

> I can't believe you saw a dragon __!__

1. When can we eat the chocolate elephant ____

2. How long did you have to wait for the ferry ____

3. Camilla just did a bungee jump ____

4. You've got a monkey on your head ____

5. You're not going to the beach, are you ____

/ 5

Each line contains two sentences. Rewrite the sentences separately with the correct punctuation at the start and end of each one. For example:

> at home I enjoy canoeing our house is by a river
> At home I enjoy canoeing. Our house is by a river.

6. can you go in the car with Suki we'll phone you when we arrive

_____

_____

/ 4

7. my dad has been bald for years luckily, the hairdresser polishes his head for free

_____

_____

/ 4

8. we're having an Easter egg hunt in the garden what time should it start

_____

_____

/ 4

Commas

Circle the incorrect comma in each sentence. For example:

Don't worry, we've got plenty(,) of time.

1. The hedgehog, which was only a baby, had been, in an accident.
2. When the sitting room, fills with light at sunset, it is delightful.
3. There was lightning that lit up the sky, thunder and, heavy rain.
4. While you're at the butcher's, can you pick up, some pork pies for lunch?
5. When I was little, I couldn't wait, until I was tall enough to go on a roller coaster.
6. The ship, which was heading for Port Arthur, struck rocks, on the way.
7. The town, which was miles from the coast, had a stone, lighthouse.

Hint: Try reading the sentences aloud — commas often go where you pause.

/ 7

Put a comma into each sentence to separate the two parts of the sentence. For example:

Until Wednesday , I had never visited the zoo before.

8. Before dinner I practised playing the accordion.
9. As we entered the maze Mum led the way towards the centre.
10. Because of my stage fright I get nervous before our concerts.
11. Despite the bad weather forecast we took a risk and went for a walk.
12. Once you've mixed in the water stir the dough for five minutes.
13. Even during the summer the rooms in the castle remain cool.
14. After you've finished painting don't forget to clean your brushes.

/ 7

Section Two — Punctuation

Apostrophes

Underline the correct word from the brackets to complete the sentence. For example:

(Kellys' <u>Kelly's</u>) team has got through to the semi-finals.

1. (**Wills'** **Will's**) dog chases him around the garden every day.

2. Kanye and Joe are taking the (**woman's** **womans'**) goat to the park.

3. The (**bird's** **birds'**) wing was injured when it hit the window.

4. Kato invited all the (**men's** **mens'**) children to the party.

5. The hockey (**player's** **players'**) lunches were ready after the match.

/ 5

Rewrite these phrases using apostrophes. For example:

the food belonging to the lion
<u>the lion's food</u>

6. the pets belonging to Marc
_____

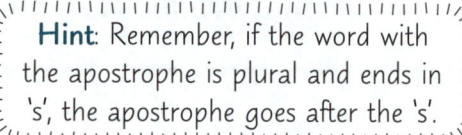

Hint: Remember, if the word with the apostrophe is plural and ends in 's', the apostrophe goes after the 's'.

7. the water belonging to the boys
_____

8. the gloves belonging to the girl
_____

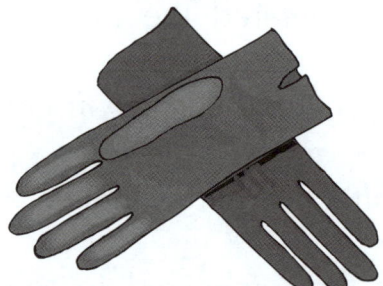

9. the paws belonging to the wolves
_____

10. the mugs belonging to the women
_____

/ 5

Apostrophes

Rewrite the words in bold in their shortened form using an apostrophe. For example:

Do not tell Katy what her birthday present is. ____Don't____

1. I **cannot** work out what I'm supposed to do. _____

2. If **you have** seen the play, you'll understand. _____

3. **I would** be delighted if the Queen asked me to tea. _____

4. **They are** happy to listen to the birds singing. _____

5. **We are** going to be late if Dad is only home at six. _____

6. The film about spider wrestling **was not** very good. _____

7. You really **should not** have gone to so much trouble. _____

/ 7

Use either **it's** or **its** to complete each sentence. For example:

____It's____ going to be a lovely day.

8. When I let the dog off _____ lead, it went crazy.

9. This milk is so old that _____ gone off.

10. Our tabby cat has lost _____ toy mouse.

Hint: If 'its' shows that something belongs to someone, it doesn't need an apostrophe.

11. The school is changing _____ uniform policy so we can wear fancy dress.

12. _____ been a long time since we went to the fair.

13. The café has opened _____ own stall in the market on Saturdays.

14. Kyle says that _____ his turn to empty the dishwasher.

/ 7

Section Two — Punctuation

Inverted Commas

Underline the words being spoken in each sentence. For example:

"<u>Would you like a cup of tea?</u>" she asked.

1. "I really want a pirate costume," said Noah.
2. "Look Gary, carrots are on offer," said Mrs Chen.
3. Mr Mackenzie shouted, "Get down off that wall!"
4. Auntie Carole asked, "How long will the roadworks go on for?"
5. "I'll have the tomato salad, please," Yottam said to the waiter.
6. "How did you get here?" asked Katherine.
7. "Look! There's a gorilla in the bath!" Jenna exclaimed.

Hint: Speech is always written inside inverted commas.

/7

Add inverted commas to complete each sentence. For example:

" Nobody will ever find out ," he muttered.

8. It's a long shot , said Pete .
9. There must be a way to escape , she whispered .
10. Basha complained , I don't want to play cricket .
11. Jump ! shouted Harish to the lady at the window .
12. I don't believe you , said Miranda .
13. The giant growled , Where's that child ?
14. We all cheered , Come on Red Team !

/7

Inverted Commas

Each sentence is missing one comma and either a question mark or a full stop. Add the missing punctuation to each sentence. For example:

" I lost five pounds , " said Robin glumly.

1. " My guinea pig ate my homework " said Arusha
2. Mum asked " How did you get so filthy "
3. Sheila muttered " Why can't you be on time "
4. " I got lost on Frencham Street " I explained
5. Tim whined " You're hogging the best skateboard "
6. " My lucky socks have spaceships on them " said Caleb

Hint: If the speech is at the end of the sentence, the full stop or question mark goes before the final inverted commas.

/ 6

Rewrite these sentences using the correct punctuation. For example:

Cliff asked why does no-one like me
Cliff asked, "Why does no-one like me?"

7. Lena whispered he didn't know that

   _____
   / 5

8. Amit declared that's Joey's little black dog

   _____
   / 5

9. Osei asked where has she hidden our presents

   _____
   / 5

10. everyone stop right now Martia shouted

    _____
    / 5

Section Two — Punctuation

Mixed Punctuation Questions

Circle the punctuation mistake in each sentence. For example:

I like to spread (B)utter in a thick layer on my toast.

1. "We've got to get out of the cellar!".

2. Our house, has six floors, twelve bedrooms and a cinema.

3. Can we swim when we get back from charlie's house?

4. "I told you to stop talking,", said Mrs Wu fiercely.

5. The monster had ten legs, blue hair and a Pink tail.

/ 5

Each of these sentences contains one punctuation error. Rewrite the sentence correctly. For example:

All the rabbit's were hiding in the burrow.
All the rabbits were hiding in the burrow.

6. my friend is moving to the Moon.

7. Sophies' car had broken down.

8. Simon was looking forward to a holiday

9. "Where are the goats? asked Jasminder.

10. "Youre the only person who knows."

/ 5

Section Two — Punctuation

Mixed Punctuation Questions

> Each of these sentences is missing one punctuation mark. Add the missing punctuation mark to each of the sentences. For example:
>
> " Please can I go out to play ? " asked Tina.

Hint: The missing punctuation marks could be full stops, question marks, exclamation marks, commas, inverted commas or apostrophes.

1. Although tennis is Stephen's favourite sport he also plays football .

2. I'm glad its Friday tomorrow as I can't wait for the weekend .

3. Hugh often says " Always look on the bright side of life . "

4. Finally it's time to present the prize for Best Film .

5. Why can't we wear skis to school

/ 5

6. My pianos pedals are going rusty .

7. You've done so well and I'm really proud , " said Grandad .

8. My new computer has speakers a mouse and lots of games .

9. " I can't believe I won ! said Chloe happily .

10. Theyre coming to visit next weekend .

/ 5

11. Although I'm only a child I like reading books about politics .

12. The gala evening raised £2000 for Uppermill Donkey Sanctuary

13. Billy has three hamsters two rabbits and a stick insect .

14. " When are we leaving I don't want to be late . "

15. The lambs fleece was beautifully white in the sunshine .

/ 5

Section Three — Spelling

Plurals

Plurals Underline the correct plural from the brackets to complete the sentence. For example:

We keep the sharp (knifes <u>knives</u>) in the top drawer.

1. Two famous (**chefs   cheves**) arrived to judge the cooking competition.

2. We'll divide the cupcake into two (**halves   halfs**).

3. The princes' (**wives   wifes**) were watching the parade together.

4. The (**shelves   shelfs**) in the bakery are full of bread.

5. The prize money was divided and stored in two separate (**safes   saves**).

6. Many people feel strongly about their (**believes   beliefs**).

7. I enjoy learning about the (**lifes   lives**) of kings and queens.

/7

Plurals Write the correct plural of the word in brackets. For example:

We played with all the ____toys____ (toy).

8. I believe in _____ (**fairy**) because I saw one in the garden.

9. All the _____ (**boy**) in my class play football at lunchtime.

10. Some _____ (**day**) in winter are very dark and gloomy.

11. There were _____ (**fly**) on the compost heap.

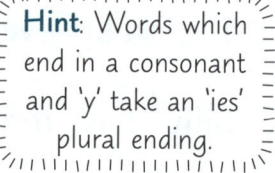

Hint: Words which end in a consonant and 'y' take an 'ies' plural ending.

12. Playing the trombone is one of my _____ (**hobby**).

13. The _____ (**pony**) are running happily around the field.

14. _____ (**Daisy**) are my favourite flower.

/7

Homophones

Underline the correct homophone from the brackets to complete each sentence. For example:

I can't (fined **find**) my red shoes.

1. My (deer **dear**) son has been studying hard.
2. I'll (**grate** great) some cheese for the pizza.
3. I think we'll have (bred **bread**) and jam for breakfast.
4. I promised that I (wood **would**) lend her my blow-up crocodile.
5. My granny used to work as a (made **maid**) at the royal palace.
6. We're going to (there **their**) holiday caravan by the sea.
7. Have you (scene **seen**) the new Wilkinson Brothers film?

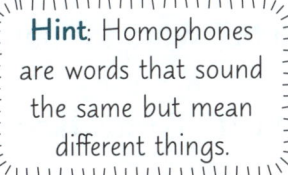
Hint: Homophones are words that sound the same but mean different things.

/ 7

Complete each sentence using **to**, **two** or **too**. For example:

We're going ___to___ their house for Christmas.

8. We're going to the shops _____ buy a goldfish.
9. I have _____ brothers called Fred and Jonny.
10. When you go to Paris, can I come _____ ?
11. Gemma didn't know how _____ unlock the safe.
12. Mira couldn't drive home because there was _____ much snow.
13. I found _____ kittens curled up next to our fireplace.
14. Salil learnt _____ ride his bike in the park.

/ 7

Section Three — Spelling

Prefixes and Suffixes

Prefixes

Underline the word with the correct prefix from the brackets to complete each sentence. For example:

The garage was an (**independent** imdependent) business.

1. Another word for naughty is (**disobedient** inobedient).

2. (**Reheat** Forheat) the soup, making sure that it's piping hot before you eat it.

3. Mustafa was very (**unkind** diskind) to me yesterday.

4. Natalie had (inusually **unusually**) bright green eyes.

5. Tina was talking (**nonsense** unsense) again.

6. Kayla can be (unpolite **impolite**) if she's not on her best behaviour.

7. I was (**unable** inable) to see over the head of the man in front.

/7

Suffixes

Add the suffix **ity**, **ion** or **ness** to the word in brackets to complete the sentence. For example:

Chi is the best gymnast because she has good __flexibility__ (**flexible**).

8. Gethin only likes watching _____ (**act**) films.

9. Iftikar sold his stamp _____ (**collect**) at the fair.

Hint: You might need to change the spelling of the word slightly when you add the suffix.

10. Sameera noticed the _____ (**similar**) between the sisters.

11. Peering through the _____ (**dark**), I could see a house among the trees.

12. The spider was filled with _____ (**sad**) when he noticed his missing leg.

13. My dad uses a satellite _____ (**navigate**) system to find his way.

14. I went canoeing at the outdoor _____ (**active**) centre.

/7

Section Three — Spelling

Awkward Spellings

Vowels

For each sentence, add a vowel to spell the word correctly.
For example:

The eleph_a_nt lived in a big field in the safari park.

1. My brother has started his own comp_____ny selling gadgets.

2. The cars were produced in the new fact_____ry.

3. My little brother was miser_____ble when it rained.

4. My mum's friend won £100 on the lott_____ry.

5. Gran gave me a wildlife calend_____r for my birthday.

6. I'll try to d_____scribe what I saw as accurately as I can.

7. Will you defin_____tely have enough time?

Hint: Vowels are 'a', 'e', 'i', 'o' and 'u'.

/ 7

Consonants

Underline the correct word from the brackets to complete each sentence. For example:

The dog (**wagged**   waged) his tail eighty times a minute.

8. He (**waded**   **wadded**) into the river to catch the fish.

9. I (**triped**   **tripped**) over and fell into the swimming pool.

10. Naomi had run out of (**wraping**   **wrapping**) paper so she used newspaper.

11. Carlos couldn't believe he had been (**chossen**   **chosen**) for the squash team.

12. Marina knew she'd been (**robed**   **robbed**) when she noticed her purse was missing.

13. Gail was (**riding**   **ridding**) her scooter when she found the abandoned car.

14. Antonio is (**thiner**   **thinner**) than the last time I saw him.

/ 7

Section Three — Spelling

Mixed Spelling Questions

> Underline the correct word to complete each sentence. For example:
>
> Her (**father** farther) likes to be called Papa.

1. I was so (**inpatient impatient**) that I couldn't wait for the party.

2. Ellie seemed to wear a (**differant different**) wig every day.

3. The (**archs arches**) in the castle are made of carved stone.

4. The kangaroo didn't pick up on the (**tension tention**) in the room.

5. (**Leafs Leaves**) turn orange and red in the autumn.

6. Mr Herbert is going to take us to pick (**blackberrys blackberries**).

7. Juliet had (**written writen**) her notes, but they had disappeared.

8. My mum said I could go out if I helped her wash the (**dishs dishes**).

9. If you lead an (**inactive unactive**) life, you may put on weight.

10. Shen started doing (**voluntry voluntary**) work when he lost his job.

11. There were lots of (**stories storys**) in Dad's book of fairy tales.

12. The mayor (**pinned pined**) a gold sticker on the winning entry.

13. I followed the (**pattern patern**), but somehow I made a shirt with three sleeves.

14. When we were in the jungle, we had to (**purify purefy**) water to drink.

15. The library was packed with (**referance reference**) books.

Mixed Spelling Questions

> Each sentence contains a spelling mistake. Underline the word with the error and write the correct spelling on the line. For example:
>
> Lilly is <u>completley</u> hopeless in the morning.   _completely_

1. What are you smileing about?   _____
2. I missread the instructions and glued my eye shut.   _____
3. The parachute landed at the foot of the cliffes.   _____
4. Don't be a coword Anton, just jump!   _____
5. The birthday cake that Mum made is barely edable.   _____

/ 5

6. Nadine is very inportant, so be polite to her.   _____
7. Do me a faver and go to the chemist's on your way.   _____
8. We both left our watchs in the changing rooms.   _____
9. It was suny so our sponsored walk was great.   _____
10. The children took there lunches to the park.   _____

/ 5

11. I couldn't decide which cloths to wear to the disco.   _____
12. The king was the most powerfull man in the land.   _____
13. George was running laps around the boundry.   _____
14. This yoghurt has no flavour; it's totally tastless.   _____
15. The bees were huming loudly inside the hive.   _____

/ 5

Section Three — Spelling

Section Four — Writers' Techniques

Alliteration and Onomatopoeia

Alliteration

Add a word to each sentence to complete the alliteration shown in bold. For example:

There was a **p**urple **p**attern on the __pottery__.

1. **S**am **s**at **s**ilently on the _____.

2. The **t**omato **t**astes _____.

3. He **p**oured a **p**int of _____ juice.

4. I **ch**ose the **ch**ips that were _____.

5. **W**endy **w**ore a _____ pair of **w**ellingtons.

6. **B**arry is a **b**ald **b**aker, who likes _____.

7. **S**paghetti **s**auce **s**pilt all over the _____.

/ 7

Onomatopoeia

Underline the onomatopoeic word in each sentence. For example:

The bee <u>buzzed</u> past my ear.

8. Somewhere in the quiet night, an owl hooted sadly.

9. Rick crashed up the rocky path to the peaceful forest.

Hint: Onomatopoeia is when a word sounds like the noise it describes.

10. The greedy pig gave a low grunt when he saw the farmer.

11. Guy trudged through the bog, his shoes squelching with every step.

12. When Oliver tripped, the silver tray he had been carrying clattered to the floor.

13. The pile of books suddenly fell to the floor with a huge thud.

14. Kalena jumped as she heard a key rattling in the rusty lock.

/ 7

Imagery

Imagery

Each sentence contains a metaphor or a simile. Write down the technique used in each sentence. For example:

> The swimmers moved like fish underwater.   __simile__

1. The football pitch was a battlefield. _____
2. The moon was a white dinner plate in the sky. _____
3. His fists were like rocks. _____
4. My brother is an animal at mealtimes. _____
5. Our kitten is a spoilt princess. _____
6. The scarecrow was as still as a statue. _____
7. Her eyes shone as bright as diamonds. _____

Hint: A simile compares one thing to something else. A metaphor says that one thing is something else.

/ 7

Imagery

Complete these similes using a suitable word. For example:

> The man was as blind as a   __bat__   .

8. The little girl was as quiet as a _____.
9. On Christmas Day, Granny was as busy as a _____.
10. During the summer, the well was as dry as a _____.
11. The door to the dungeon was as solid as a _____.
12. When Mum is angry, her expression is as cold as _____.
13. The newborn baby was as light as a _____.
14. When she heard the news, she went as white as a _____.

/ 7

Section Four — Writers' Techniques

Synonyms

Underline the word in each question that has the most similar meaning to the word in bold. For example:

start   slow   stop   <u>begin</u>   fast

1. **mend**   hurt   fix   break   replace
2. **jolly**   satisfied tired   nervous   happy
3. **concerned**   careful   dangerous worried   excited
4. **sea**   lake   river   ocean   pond
5. **clever**   generous   keen   kind   intelligent
6. **silly**   wrong   wise   foolish   mistaken
7. **glossy**   rough   shiny   peaceful   flat

Hint: Words with very similar meanings are called synonyms.

/ 7

Underline the word from the brackets that has the most similar meaning to the word in bold. For example:

The palace was very **pretty**. (<u>attractive</u> spooky grand)

8. It was getting late and I was starting to feel **tired**. (bright sleepy old)

9. Mrs Watson liked to go **jogging** after work. (cycling swimming running)

10. Karen hid in the **cupboard** and watched David search. (stool cabinet table)

11. Dr Savania was a good doctor because he was **caring**. (helpful polite kind)

12. Magnus **jumped** off the creaky diving board into the pool. (ran leapt climbed)

13. Timothy **watched** his favourite film again. (looked viewed tried)

14. Melanie was **uneasy** about moving to Nepal. (nervous excited afraid)

/ 7

Section Four — Writers' Techniques

Antonyms

Underline the word in each question that has the opposite meaning to the word in bold. For example:

hot   windy   cool   <u>cold</u>   wet

1. **tame**   alive   wild   escaped   home
2. **frowning** pleased smiling angry   bored
3. **elderly**   old   young   aged   active
4. **near**   close   wide   distant   short
5. **old**   clean   expensive new   scruffy
6. **ill**   poorly   sick   cheerful   healthy
7. **clean**   broken   dirty   natural   perfect

Hint: Words with opposite meanings are called antonyms.

/ 7

Underline the word from the brackets that has the opposite meaning to the word in bold. For example:

Fabio wondered when the concert would **start**. (<u>end</u> begin last)

8. Our next-door neighbour's cat is **bald**. (ginger soft hairy)

9. Priya left **early** for her audition. (late punctually before)

10. Mick didn't want to **blame** her for what had happened. (give praise hate)

11. The idea behind the plan is **simple**, so it should work. (right complex OK)

12. My Aunty Sheila has a wide circle of **friends**. (companions family enemies)

13. I would really like to **succeed** in my new job. (win fail bad)

14. The room looked **appealing**. (rich familiar disgusting)

/ 7

Section Four — Writers' Techniques

Section Five — Writing

Creative Writing

Adjectives

Replace the word in bold with a different adjective which has a stronger meaning. For example:

The new baby is **small**.   _tiny_

1. The play we went to see was **bad**. _____
2. Aditi packed a **big** suitcase for her holiday. _____
3. Polar bears live in **cold** conditions. _____
4. The pink silk dress was **pretty**. _____
5. We were **pleased** to hear the good news. _____
6. My great-grandma is **old**. _____
7. Nerissa made a **tasty** pizza. _____

/ 7

Speech

Each of these sentences contains some speech. Complete each sentence without using the word "said". For example:

"Put your chairs under your desks," _instructed_ the teacher.

8. "How long will you be in town?" _____ Ariel.
9. "I'll be really well behaved if you bring me a present," _____ Theo.
10. "Perhaps we could go down to the arcade together," _____ Amy.
11. "But I don't want to do my homework," _____ Arthur.
12. "You can't do that!" Krys _____.
13. "Smithson, bring me the map now," _____ the general.
14. "My leg is bleeding," _____ the wounded policeman.

/ 7

Creative Writing

Write two sentences describing each of the following things.
Use adjectives to make your writing interesting. For example:

> What your house looks like:
> <u>My house is semi-detached with a dark blue front door.</u>
> <u>It is built from red bricks and has a sloping roof.</u>

1. What the town or village where you live is like:

   _____

   _____

   _____   / 2

2. What the weather was like yesterday:

   _____

   _____

   _____   / 2

3. What your school is like:

   _____

   _____

   _____   / 2

4. What you did for your last birthday:

   _____

   _____

   _____   / 2

Section Five — Writing

Non-Fiction Writing

You can improve your writing by understanding the purpose of different texts. Write down whether each of these sentences is persuading (P) or informing (I). For example:

> You should try Emma's gingerbread; it's the best in town.   P

Hint: Persuasive writing often uses lots of adjectives to try to appeal to the reader's emotions.

1. Watch Robo-cat, the crime-fighting supercat, on channel 2 this Saturday! _____

2. Queen Elizabeth I was Queen of England for more than 40 years. _____

3. Blue whales live in the ocean and are the largest animals on Earth. _____

4. Try ballroom dancing because it's lots of fun and a great way to stay fit. _____

5. This Christmas, buy the new Flying Fox which lets you fly to school! _____

6. In Iceland, the phone book is organised by people's first names. _____

/ 6

Write a sentence persuading a friend to do each of the following tasks. For example:

> To read your favourite book:
> *You must read this book because it has an exciting ending.*

7. To come to your birthday party:

_____

/ 2

8. To go for a picnic at the weekend:

_____

/ 2

Section Five — Writing

Non-Fiction Writing

These short passages describe a task in the past tense. Rewrite each passage as a set of instructions in the present tense for someone doing the same task. The first instruction has been done for you.

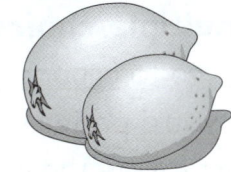

Hint: Think about how you would tell someone to do something if you were speaking.

1. **Making lemonade:**
   I took three lemons and squeezed them. I stirred sugar into the lemon juice. I poured fizzy water over the lemon and sugar. I mixed the lemonade well. I poured it into a jug and I added a slice of lemon to decorate it.

   Take three lemons and squeeze them.

   / 4

2. **Catching the bus:**
   I walked to the bus stop. I waited for bus number 36. I got on the bus and asked for a single ticket to the library. I paid £1.70 and sat down on the bus. I pressed the button to let the bus driver know that I wanted to stop at the library.

   Walk to the bus stop.

   / 4

Assessment Test 1

This book contains eight assessment tests, which get harder as you work through them to help you improve your English skills.

Allow 30 minutes to do each test and work as quickly and as carefully as you can.

If you want to attempt each test more than once, you will need to print **multiple-choice answer sheets** for these questions from our website — go to cgpbooks.co.uk/11plus/answer-sheets or scan the QR code on the right. If you'd prefer to answer the questions on the page, just follow the instructions in the question.

Answer Sheets

> Read this passage carefully and answer the questions that follow.

The Dinosaur Dipper

Sanjay and his dad had been waiting in the queue for the roller coaster for a long time. Bored, Sanjay tugged Dad's sleeve, "Are we nearly at the front?"
When the family had arrived at the theme park that morning they'd bought their tickets from a friendly lady who was dressed as a cavewoman. When they
5 walked through the gates of the theme park, the Dinosaur Dipper roller coaster was the first thing Sanjay had seen. It towered over the other rides, its shiny green track looping high above the ground. Brightly painted carriages zoomed along the tracks, and the passengers' excited cries echoed through the air.
"Can we go on that ride, Dad?" Sanjay had begged. "Please?"
10 "Be patient," Dad had replied. "We're going to take Maya on some smaller rides first." Maya was Sanjay's baby sister. She was only three, but she was running around and shouting excitedly because she was happy to be out of her pram.
Finally, Dad and Sanjay had left Maya and Mum at the café and made their way towards the Dinosaur Dipper, where they had queued for what seemed like hours.
15 All of a sudden, the queue in front of them surged forwards, and Sanjay saw an official-looking man helping people onto the ride. Sanjay watched a group of teenagers climb excitedly into the colourful carriages. They chatted and giggled as they strapped the safety belts on tightly. With a loud clang and a clatter, the carriages shot forward.
20 Sanjay felt butterflies in his stomach. Suddenly the ride seemed very high and very fast. He wasn't sure that it looked fun after all. Before Sanjay could say anything, Dad turned around and took his hand.
"Come on, it's our turn!" he said.
The crowd hurried forward and Sanjay was swept through the gate. Dad led
25 him towards a carriage with a huge grin on his face.
"This is going to be fun!"

Assessment Test 1

Answer these questions about the text that you've just read.
Circle the letter that matches the correct answer.

1. What did Sanjay see when he first entered the theme park?

    A Lots of people
    B The gift shop
    C Some smaller rides
    D The Dinosaur Dipper
    E The café

2. Why did Sanjay not go on the Dinosaur Dipper straight away?

    A He was frightened.
    B He didn't think it looked fun.
    C Maya wanted to go on it later.
    D The queue was too long.
    E They took Maya on some other rides first.

3. Who did Sanjay see while he was waiting in the queue for the roller coaster?

    A A man selling ice creams
    B One of his friends from school
    C A man checking tickets
    D People taking photographs
    E Someone helping people onto the ride

4. Which of the following statements is not true?

    A Sanjay and his dad queued for the ride for a long time.
    B The teenagers ahead of Sanjay put on their safety belts.
    C The teenagers ahead of Sanjay were nervous about the ride.
    D The ride made a loud sound as it set off.
    E The carriages moved very quickly when the ride set off.

5. Which of these two words describe the Dinosaur Dipper?

    A Bright and colourful
    B Boring and empty
    C Tall and slow
    D Small and loopy
    E Fast and straight

/ 5

Carry on to the next question → →

Assessment Test 1

Answer these questions about the text that you've just read.
Circle the letter that matches the correct answer.

6. What does Sanjay think about the roller coaster when he reaches the end of the queue?
   A He thinks it might break down.
   B He thinks it will be really boring.
   C He thinks it won't be very enjoyable.
   D He thinks it will be exciting.
   E He thinks it looks like a ride for small children.

7. Where is Maya while Sanjay and his dad are waiting to get on the Dinosaur Dipper?
   A On a smaller ride
   B With Mum in the café
   C On the roller coaster already
   D In the queue with them
   E In the ticket office with Mum

/ 2

Answer these questions about the way words and phrases are used in the passage.

8. Which of these words is closest in meaning to "tugged" (line 2)?
   A Touched
   B Pulled
   C Pushed
   D Moaned
   E Helped

9. Which of these words is closest in meaning to "chatted" (line 17)?
   A Smiled
   B Whispered
   C Shouted
   D Talked
   E Laughed

10. What is meant by the expression "Sanjay was swept through the gate" (line 24)?
    A Sanjay was pushed through the gate quickly.
    B Sanjay fell over before he reached the gate.
    C Sanjay walked calmly through the gate.
    D Sanjay turned around and left the queue.
    E Sanjay jumped over the gate.

/ 3

Assessment Test 1

Answer these questions about the way words and phrases are used in the passage.

11. What type of words are "echoed" (line 8) and "begged" (line 9)?
    - A Nouns
    - B Adverbs
    - C Adjectives
    - D Verbs
    - E Similes

12. "Dad led him towards a carriage with a huge grin on his face" (lines 24-25). Which of these words is an adjective?
    - A Dad
    - B towards
    - C carriage
    - D huge
    - E grin

/ 2

Choose the right word or phrase to fill the gap.
Circle the letter which matches the correct word.

13. Yesterday, Jen **ask say told speak telled** me all about the day she spent with
             A B C D E

14. Malik. She had asked me to go with them, but I **not couldn't do can would** go
             A B C D E

15. because I **are has will had is** to stay in to help my mum. Jen described the den
         A B C D E

16. they made in the woods. First, they tied a rope **until since between in though**
             A B C D E

17. two trees **and if while because soon** then put a plastic sheet over it. Next, they
         A B C D E

18. collected sticks and twigs **by if to so and** cover the sheet so it would blend
            A B C D E

19. into the trees. **Finally First Second But Once**, they put dried leaves on the
             A B C D E

20. floor of the den and **sat seated sitting seat sit** in it all afternoon.
             A B C D E

/ 8

Carry on to the next question → →

Assessment Test 1

In each sentence, there is one punctuation mistake. Circle the letter which matches the part of the sentence with the mistake.

21. Fran made a giant white chocolate and raspberry cake for her older brother's birthday?
    A B C D E

22. "Shut up! shouted Mum angrily when the boys started to argue over the last ice lolly.
    A B C D E

23. I would'nt have believed that it was true if I hadn't seen it happen with my own eyes.
    A B C D E

24. While I was in London, I went to Buckingham Palace with, my friends Anne and John.
    A B C D E

25. The three naughty girl's quickly ran down the street, turned the corner and disappeared.
    A B C D E

/ 5

In each sentence, there is one spelling mistake. Circle the letter which matches the part of the sentence with the mistake.

26. The brave explorer slowly and carefully wallked across the rocky, narrow ledge to safety.
    A B C D E

27. George gave his sister a generous peace of chocolate cake and a big glass of lemonade.
    A B C D E

28. Edwin wasn't as good as Hasan at tennis, but he could eassely beat him at badminton.
    A B C D E

29. After a lot of thought, Julia decided to buy a skirt because the weather was so suny.
    A B C D E

30. The children all had a wonderfull time on their holiday in the south of Spain.
    A B C D E

/ 5

Total / 30

End of Test

Assessment Test 1

Assessment Test 2

Allow 30 minutes to do this test and work as quickly and as carefully as you can.

You can print **multiple-choice answer sheets** for these questions from our website — go to cgpbooks.co.uk/11plus/answer-sheets or scan the QR code on the right. If you'd prefer to answer the questions on the page, just follow the instructions in the question.

Read this passage carefully and answer the questions that follow.

Thank you letter

Dear Aunt Angela,
    I am writing to thank you for the present you gave me. I opened it on Christmas morning, but I must confess that I had peeled back a corner of the wrapping paper two days before. I had just got home from school and Mum was on the phone to Aunt
5 Glenda, so while her back was turned, I gave all my presents under the tree a squeeze. I could guess what most of them were, but I couldn't resist a quick peek at the one from you. When Mum saw that part of the paper had been ripped off she was furious and accused me of doing it, but I managed to convince her that Poppy had scratched it with her claws.
10   When I was finally allowed to open your present, I pretended to be surprised. I think I should have been given an award for my acting! I tore into the wrapping paper like a wild animal and gave a dramatic gasp when I opened it.
    I couldn't wait to play with your gift. I rushed into the garden, even though it was raining, and set up a goal post. I wanted to use Grandad's walking sticks, but they
15 wouldn't stand up by themselves, so I had to use one of Dad's garden gnomes and an upturned flowerpot instead. It was windy, so my first shot missed the goal by a mile and ended up near the shed, but my second shot hit the target fair and square! I ran around with my arms in the air to celebrate, just like the footballers on the television.
    Thanks again for the new football. It was definitely my favourite Christmas
20 present this year.

Love from,
Anita

Answer these questions about the text that you've just read.
Circle the letter that matches the correct answer.

1. What was the weather like when Anita went into the garden?

    A It was windy and snowing.
    B The air was still and it was sunny.
    C The wind was blowing and it was raining.
    D It was raining and cold.
    E It was cold and sunny.

2. Why did Anita pretend to be surprised when she opened Aunt Angela's present?

    A Anita didn't like the present.
    B Someone had told Anita what was inside.
    C Poppy had already ripped off the wrapping paper.
    D Aunt Angela bought Anita the same gift every year.
    E Anita had already seen part of the present.

3. Which of these words best describes the way that Anita opened Aunt Angela's present?

    A Quickly
    B Carefully
    C Slowly
    D Nervously
    E Curiously

4. When did Anita try to guess what the presents were?

    A Before school
    B After dinner
    C Late at night
    D After school
    E Before her bath

5. Who do you think Poppy is?

    A Anita's big sister
    B Anita's aunt
    C Anita's next-door neighbour
    D Anita's pet
    E Anita's little sister

/ 5

Assessment Test 2

Answer these questions about the text that you've just read.
Circle the letter that matches the correct answer.

6. What did Anita use as a goal?

    A   Poppy and a gnome
    B   A flowerpot and a gnome
    C   The shed
    D   The fence
    E   Grandad's walking sticks

7. Where did Anita's first shot go?

    A   On the shed roof
    B   Into the Christmas tree
    C   Near the shed
    D   In the next-door neighbour's garden
    E   In the goal

/ 2

Answer these questions about the way words and phrases are used in the passage.

8. Which of these words is closest in meaning to "ripped" (line 7)?

    A   Mended
    B   Smashed
    C   Torn
    D   Hurt
    E   Stolen

9. Which of these words is closest in meaning to "furious" (line 7)?

    A   Distracted
    B   Sad
    C   Disappointed
    D   Pleased
    E   Angry

10. Which of these words is closest in meaning to "surprised" (line 10)?

    A   Bored
    B   Annoyed
    C   Pleased
    D   Shocked
    E   Upset

/ 3

Carry on to the next question → →

Answer these questions about the way words and phrases are used in the passage.

11. "I tore into the wrapping paper like a wild animal" (lines 11-12).
    What technique is this an example of?

    A A metaphor
    B A simile
    C A synonym
    D Alliteration
    E A homophone

12. "my first shot missed the goal by a mile" (line 16).
    Which of these words is a verb?

    A first
    B shot
    C missed
    D by
    E mile

/ 2

In each sentence, there is one spelling mistake. Circle the letter which matches the part of the sentence with the mistake.

13. Nobody herd the thief as he sneaked through the open window of the empty house.
       A   B   C   D   E

14. I could not sleep last night because the babys were crying and wailing until midnight.
        A   B   C   D   E

15. Nirav's sister was allmost tall enough to reach the top shelf of the kitchen cupboard.
          A   B   C   D   E

16. Joby was really looking forward to the tastey Sunday lunch at his grandma's house.
         A   B   C   D   E

17. "You certainly won't be able to get there if you don't now the way," warned Donna.
            A   B   C   D   E

18. The teacher explained how to use the sissors so the children wouldn't cut themselves.
            A   B   C   D   E

19. The Dion family had to move house last year because of the terrable floods.
           A   B   C   D   E

20. Tariq wrote the adress for Mary's flat with a pencil on a piece of scrap paper.
         A   B   C   D   E

/ 8

Assessment Test 2

> Choose the right word or phrase to fill the gap.
> Circle the letter which matches the correct word.

21. We watched the startled family of **deer** (A) **deers** (B) **deeres** (C) **deeries** (D) **dear** (E) run into the

22. forest. As we walked away, **us** (A) **our** (B) **my** (C) **I** (D) **me** (E) noticed that one of the animals

23. was still nearby. It was **drink** (A) **thirsty** (B) **drank** (C) **drinking** (D) **dranked** (E) from a puddle

24. and hadn't **look** (A) **saw** (B) **looked** (C) **sees** (D) **seen** (E) us. When it looked up, it froze for a

25. second before running **after** (A) **away** (B) **quickly** (C) **slowly** (D) **off** (E) its family.

/ 5

> In each sentence, there is one punctuation mistake. Circle the letter which matches the part of the sentence with the mistake.

26. "What is the point (A) of using punctuation (B) properly!" (C) asked Robert (D) with a huge grin. (E)

27. The chocolate cake (A) had risen perfectly and (B) Rita thought that (C) it looked ready (D) to be iced (E)

28. If I'd known, (A) how tired you were (B) going to be (C) after work, I'd have (D) cooked dinner myself. (E)

29. Yvonnes washing (A) was all over (B) the garden (C) and in the street (D) because of the strong wind. (E)

30. Naava visited (A) a wonderful old Castle (B) during the school's (C) annual summer trip (D) to Wales. (E)

/ 5

Total / 30

End of Test

Assessment Test 2

Assessment Test 3

Allow 30 minutes to do this test and work as quickly and as carefully as you can.

You can print **multiple-choice answer sheets** for these questions from our website — go to cgpbooks.co.uk/11plus/answer-sheets or scan the QR code on the right. If you'd prefer to answer the questions on the page, just follow the instructions in the question.

Read this passage carefully and answer the questions that follow.

Roger's Records

"Dad?"
"What now?" Roger's father said wearily, without looking up from his newspaper.
"Guess how old Robert Wadlow was when he could carry his father up the stairs."
"I've no idea," said Roger's father.
5   "Have a guess," Roger insisted.
"Twelve."
"Wrong! It says here that Robert Pershing Wadlow, the tallest man that ever lived, was nine years old. That's the same age as me!"
Mr Cherry had been forced to listen to many of these fascinating facts from
10 his son, but he had only himself to blame. It was his idea to buy Roger his first 'Book of World Records' three years ago and he had given his son the new edition every Christmas since then.
"Dad?"
"Yes, son."
15 "What do you think the record is for the furthest distance for spitting a watermelon seed?"
"Ten metres," said Mr Cherry, reading the same sentence in his newspaper for the fifth time.
"Wrong! It's actually seventy three metres!" yelled Roger triumphantly.
20 He loved it when his father got the answer wrong. He was a teacher but he didn't know his records. Roger searched for another killer question. He knew that he probably only had time for one more before his father's patience ran out. He started reading about the woman with the longest fingernails in the world.
"Dad?"
25 There was no reply. Roger looked across the living room at an outspread newspaper that seemed to have sprouted legs and feet. The feet were wearing tartan slippers, and coming from behind the newspaper was a sound like the breathing of a wounded warthog. Roger wondered if there was a record for the loudest snoring in the world!

Answer these questions about the text that you've just read.
Circle the letter that matches the correct answer.

1. How old is Roger?

    A Six
    B Seven
    C Eight
    D Nine
    E Ten

2. According to the text, what could Robert Pershing Wadlow do?

    A Carry his father up the stairs
    B Spit watermelon seeds
    C Grow really long finger nails
    D Tell his father annoying facts
    E Snore louder than anyone else in the world

3. When does Roger receive each year's 'Book of World Records'?

    A On his birthday
    B At Christmas
    C Every January
    D At Easter
    E When he has been good

4. What is Roger's father's job?

    A Journalist
    B Teacher
    C Writer for the 'Book of World Records'
    D Policeman
    E Builder

5. Which word best describes how Roger's father feels about Roger's questions?

    A Confused
    B Proud
    C Furious
    D Happy
    E Uninterested

/ 5

Carry on to the next question → →

Assessment Test 3

Answer these questions about the text that you've just read.
Circle the letter that matches the correct answer.

6. Which of these records is not mentioned in the story?

   A The World's furthest seed spit
   B The World's tallest man
   C The World's longest fingernails
   D The World's best-selling book
   E The World's loudest snore

7. Why does Roger's father not reply to Roger's final question?

   A He has already left the room.
   B He refuses to answer any more questions.
   C He has fallen asleep.
   D He is concentrating on reading.
   E He is watching a cartoon on television.

/ 2

Answer these questions about the way words and phrases are used in the passage.

8. Which of these words is closest in meaning to "yelled" (line 19)?

   A Shouted
   B Laughed
   C Said
   D Whispered
   E Begged

9. Which of these words is closest in meaning to "fascinating" (line 9)?

   A Wrong
   B Boring
   C Out-of-date
   D Interesting
   E Correct

10. Which of these words is closest in meaning to "sprouted" (line 26)?

    A Appeared
    B Walked
    C Lost
    D Grown
    E Eaten

/ 3

Assessment Test 3

Answer these questions about the way words and phrases are used in the passage.

11. "a sound like the breathing of a wounded warthog" (lines 27-28).
    Which of the following words is an adjective?
    - A sound
    - B like
    - C breathing
    - D wounded
    - E warthog

12. "Roger" (line 5) and "Christmas" (line 12) are examples of which part of speech?
    - A Common nouns
    - B Verbs
    - C Adjectives
    - D Proper nouns
    - E Pronouns

/ 2

In each sentence, there is one punctuation mistake. Circle the letter which matches the part of the sentence with the mistake.

13. The boys' mother took Them both to the cinema to see a film called 'Star Battle Heroes'.
    A   B   C   D   E

14. "I'm sure that you'll really enjoy yourself if you come with us to play in the park?"
    A   B   C   D   E

15. The ingredients I need to make the cake are flour, butter, sugar eggs and skimmed milk.
    A   B   C   D   E

16. "I'm going to leave on Wednesday morning," he said, although nobody believed him".
    A   B   C   D   E

17. Hannah and her family lived in a small house in the village of oakthorpe.
    A   B   C   D   E

18. Raj's grandfather cant' wait to retire because it means that he'll get a free bus pass.
    A   B   C   D   E

19. Great Britain's population is more than 60 million and it continues to, grow every day.
    A   B   C   D   E

20. "Have you ever been on holiday to France, Italy, Austria or Spain? asked Gina.
    A   B   C   D   E

/ 8

Carry on to the next question → →

Assessment Test 3

> In each sentence, there is one spelling mistake. Circle the letter which matches the part of the sentence with the mistake.

21. The teacher did not believe Feng's exscuse for not doing her weekly science homework.
    A   B   C   D   E

22. They were forty kilometres from their destinasion when the train came to a sudden halt.
    A   B   C   D   E

23. While most of the children ran accross the yard, Rosie preferred to hop on one leg.
    A   B   C   D   E

24. I wish that Gabriella would stop asking questions because it's nun of her business!
    A   B   C   D   E

25. When the alarm rang, the children kept carm and left the building quickly and quietly.
    A   B   C   D   E

/ 5

> Choose the right word or phrase to fill the gap. Circle the letter which matches the correct word.

26. When we went to the zoo on Friday, I saw **a an some two none** elephant. It was
    A B   C   D   E

27. bigger than I **has had is will am** imagined. As we watched, it started
    A   B   C   D   E

28. playing in a large pond **by up between down far** the fence. After a few
    A B   C   D   E

29. minutes, the elephant **begin beginned start begunned began** to spray
    A   B   C   D   E

30. water over the crowd! The zookeeper could **be no of not to** stop laughing.
    A B C D E

/ 5

Total / 30

End of Test

Assessment Test 3

Assessment Test 4

Allow 30 minutes to do this test and work as quickly and as carefully as you can.

You can print **multiple-choice answer sheets** for these questions from our website — go to cgpbooks.co.uk/11plus/answer-sheets or scan the QR code on the right. If you'd prefer to answer the questions on the page, just follow the instructions in the question.

Read this passage carefully and answer the questions that follow.

Castles

After the Normans invaded England in 1066, they immediately started to build castles all around the country. These castles were not just ordinary buildings, but were fortresses to protect Norman soldiers from their enemies.
The earliest Norman castles were either made within an existing Roman
5 fort or were 'motte and bailey' castles. The word 'motte' means a natural or man-made mound and the word 'bailey' means an enclosure. The bailey was a yard area which was surrounded by a wall. These castles were built by local peasants and could be constructed quickly. Once they had dug a deep, circular ditch, they piled the earth from the ditch into the centre to form the high hill
10 known as the motte. A wooden building called a 'keep' was built on top of the motte as a look-out point. The keep was at the top of the motte, so it would have been difficult for enemy troops to attack it. The deep ditch around the castle also helped to protect it from invaders.
A courtyard was built next to the motte, and this was known as the bailey.
15 There were many buildings within the bailey, including stables, storerooms, kitchens and living quarters. Many of the castle's workers lived and worked inside the bailey. The bailey was often surrounded by a palisade. This was a tall fence made using wooden stakes and was an important part of the castle's defence.
Motte and bailey castles were quick and cheap to build and provided good
20 defence against the enemy. However, they were built out of wood, so they caught fire easily. Over time, people started building castles out of stone because they lasted longer and to prevent them from burning down.

Answer these questions about the text that you've just read.
Circle the letter that matches the correct answer.

1. According to the text, what is a 'bailey'?

   A   A hill
   B   A courtyard
   C   A fortress
   D   A Roman soldier
   E   A castle

2. Which of the following was an important part of the castle's defence?

   A   The bailey
   B   The kitchens
   C   The palisade
   D   Local peasants
   E   The wooden buildings

3. Which of the following is not given as a reason why the Normans built motte and bailey castles?

   A   They were very big.
   B   They were quick to build.
   C   They were difficult to attack.
   D   They were cheap to build.
   E   They provided good defence.

4. According to the text, which of the following buildings was not in the bailey?

   A   The kitchens
   B   The stables
   C   Living quarters
   D   Storerooms
   E   The school

5. Which of the following does not describe a 'motte'?

   A   A natural mound
   B   A heap of earth
   C   A high hill
   D   A Roman fort
   E   Part of a castle

/ 5

Assessment Test 4

Answer these questions about the text that you've just read.
Circle the letter that matches the correct answer.

6. According to the text, what was the purpose of the castle's 'keep'?

   A To attack from
   B To keep animals in
   C To store weapons in
   D To watch for enemies
   E To walk around

7. According to the passage, why were later castles built out of stone instead of wood?

   A Stone was cheaper.
   B Wood was running out.
   C There was more stone available.
   D Wood could catch fire.
   E Stone was difficult to attack.

/ 2

Answer these questions about the way words and phrases are used in the passage.

8. Which of these words is closest in meaning to "prevent" (line 22)?

   A Help
   B Watch
   C Rescue
   D Stop
   E Go

9. Which of these words is closest in meaning to "invaders" (line 13)?

   A Armies
   B Attackers
   C Friends
   D Defenders
   E Builders

10. Which of these words is closest in meaning to "circular" (line 8)?

    A Long
    B Round
    C Around
    D Wide
    E Smooth

/ 3

Carry on to the next question → →

Assessment Test 4

Answer these questions about the way words and phrases are used in the passage.

11. "they were built out of wood, so they caught fire easily" (lines 20-21).
    Which of these words is an adverb?

    A they
    B built
    C wood
    D fire
    E easily

12. "deep" (line 8) and "cheap" (line 19) are examples of which part of speech?

    A Adjectives
    B Adverbs
    C Nouns
    D Verbs
    E Pronouns

/ 2

In each sentence, there is one spelling mistake. Circle the letter which matches the part of the sentence with the mistake.

13. Elliot always rushs his homework so that he can go and play rugby with his friends.
    A   B   C   D   E

14. Matilda couldn't believe that Bruce had eaten the hole chocolate cake in one go.
    A   B   C   D   E

15. Their was enough time to make sure that all the children had a turn on the trampoline.
    A   B   C   D   E

16. The female community choir won seccond place in the national talent show.
    A   B   C   D   E

17. Sumana ran straight threw the hall and out into the playground without stopping.
    A   B   C   D   E

18. The whether was fine so the family decided to have a picnic in the park at lunchtime.
    A   B   C   D   E

19. Mario was feeling very energetick, so he went for a long run before he played hockey.
    A   B   C   D   E

20. Nafisa had been expecting a bycycle so the present wasn't much of a surprise.
    A   B   C   D   E

/ 8

Assessment Test 4

In each sentence, there is one punctuation mistake. Circle the letter which matches the part of the sentence with the mistake.

21. "do you think Diana will arrive in time for the last train to Beverley?" asked Anne.
    A   B   C   D   E

22. Billy, Salim, john, Kyle, Harry and Kim all turned up late for their science class.
        A   B   C   D   E

23. Even though theres heavy snow, they still want to play football in the park.
         A   B   C   D   E

24. "Have you seen my new blue coat" asked Ewa, looking around the room sadly.
         A   B   C   D   E

25. Georgina took a deep breath and then yelled, Ready or not, here I come!"
         A   B   C   D   E

/ 5

Choose the right word or phrase to fill the gap.
Circle the letter which matches the correct word.

26. "Can I have **a one some few an** grapes, please?" asked Mrs Rhency. Mr Apple,
              A B   C   D   E

27. the greengrocer, took a bunch from a shelf **behind across between through to**
                                                 A   B   C   D   E

28. him. He smiled at Mrs Rhency, who **are were will be has was** his favourite
                                        A   B   C   D   E

29. customer. She **byes bought buy brings bys** all her fruit and vegetables from
                    A   B   C   D   E

30. him **even too with and if** she usually had a piece of local gossip to tell him.
         A   B   C   D   E

/ 5

Total / 30

End of Test

Assessment Test 4

Assessment Test 5

Allow 30 minutes to do this test and work as quickly and as carefully as you can.

You can print **multiple-choice answer sheets** for these questions from our website — go to cgpbooks.co.uk/11plus/answer-sheets or scan the QR code on the right. If you'd prefer to answer the questions on the page, just follow the instructions in the question.

Read this poem carefully and answer the questions that follow.

The Fieldmouse

Where the acorn tumbles down,
Where the ash tree sheds its berry,
With your fur so soft and brown,
With your eye so round and merry,
5   Scarcely moving the long grass,
Fieldmouse, I can see you pass.

Little thing, in what dark den,
Lie you all the winter sleeping?
Till warm weather comes again,
10 Then once more I see you peeping
Round about the tall tree roots,
Nibbling at their fallen fruits.

Fieldmouse, fieldmouse, do not go,
Where the farmer stacks his treasure,
15 Find the nut that falls below,
Eat the acorn at your pleasure,
But you must not steal the grain
He has stacked with so much pain.

Make your hole where mosses spring,
20 Underneath the tall oak's shadow,
Pretty, quiet harmless thing,
Play about the sunny meadow.
Keep away from corn and house,
None will harm you, little mouse.

by Cecil Frances Alexander

Answer these questions about the text that you've just read.
Circle the letter that matches the correct answer.

1. What does the fieldmouse do in the winter?

    A   It sleeps in a dark den.
    B   It moves somewhere warmer.
    C   It stores nuts and fruit.
    D   It plays in the meadow.
    E   It eats lots of food.

2. According to the poem, what should the fieldmouse not eat?

    A   Acorns
    B   Fruits
    C   Tree roots
    D   Berries
    E   Corn

3. Which of these words best describes the fieldmouse?

    A   Fat and happy
    B   Sad and anxious
    C   Pretty and gentle
    D   Harmful and noisy
    E   Hungry and tired

4. Which of these statements about the farmer is true?

    A   He is very rich.
    B   He stores grain.
    C   He is ill.
    D   He is sleepy.
    E   He is merry.

5. Where does the poet tell the fieldmouse to make its den in verse 4?

    A   In the long grass
    B   Under the ash tree
    C   Under the oak tree
    D   In the meadow
    E   Inside the house

/ 5

Carry on to the next question → →

Answer these questions about the text that you've just read.
Circle the letter that matches the correct answer.

6. Which of these does the fieldmouse not do?

   A Find food
   B Eat
   C Play
   D Go to the farmer's house
   E Make a nest

7. Why does the fieldmouse "scarcely" (line 5) move the grass?

   A Because the fieldmouse is so small
   B Because the fieldmouse's fur is so soft
   C Because the grass is so heavy
   D Because the fieldmouse is so fast
   E Because the fieldmouse is sleeping

/ 2

Answer these questions about the way words and phrases are used in the poem.

8. Which of these words is closest in meaning to "nibbling" (line 12)?

   A Chewing
   B Chattering
   C Gulping
   D Looking
   E Destroying

9. Which of these words is closest in meaning to "stacks" (line 14)?

   A Produces
   B Scatters
   C Sells
   D Counts
   E Heaps

10. Which of these words is closest in meaning to "sheds" (line 2)?

    A Huts
    B Grows
    C Drops
    D Finds
    E Shows

/ 3

Assessment Test 5

Answer these questions about the way words and phrases are used in the poem.

11. What type of words are "soft" (line 3) and "merry" (line 4)?
    - A Verbs
    - B Nouns
    - C Adverbs
    - D Adjectives
    - E Pronouns

12. "Find the nut that falls below" (line 15).
    Which of these words is a verb?
    - A Find
    - B the
    - C nut
    - D that
    - E below

/ 2

Choose the right word or phrase to fill the gap.
Circle the letter which matches the correct word.

13. Today we are **going   go   to   goes   went** shopping for decorations for my party.
                      A   B   C   D   E

14. Hopefully we'll be able to buy some pirate flags **or   why   because   therefore   then**
                                                           A   B   C   D   E

15. I'm having a pirate party. Everyone is going to **were   ware   where   wear   wears**
                                                         A   B   C   D   E

16. fancy dress. I've got an eyepatch and a sword, and I **are   is   am   have   been** going
                                                                A B C D E

17. to paint a beard on my face **for   too   two   as   to** . Mum has booked a bouncy castle,
                                       A B   C   D E

18. and Dad is baking a birthday cake. I haven't decided **what   when   how   who   that**
                                                              A   B   C   D   E

19. I'm going to invite yet, **and   or   but   if   when** my best friends Loreen, Ravi and
                                      A   B   C   D   E

20. Peter have **saying   says   speak   say   said** that they've already bought their outfits.
                    A   B   C   D   E

/ 8

Carry on to the next question → →

Assessment Test 5

> In each sentence, there is one punctuation mistake. Circle the letter which matches the part of the sentence with the mistake.

21. Wild animals like hedgehogs owls and deer can all be found at the rescue centre.
    A — B — C — D — E

22. "How many lengths of the pool did you swim" Liam asked his older brother.
    A — B — C — D — E

23. "Please put the tablecloth on the table ready for the cake sale, Joya said politely.
    A — B — C — D — E

24. My teacher, mr Gerard, has organised a concert and a play at the community centre.
    A — B — C — D — E

25. If its raining over the weekend, Mum says she'll take us bowling and to the cinema.
    A — B — C — D — E

/ 5

> In each sentence, there is one spelling mistake. Circle the letter which matches the part of the sentence with the mistake.

26. When Abdullah woke up, he polished his new bicycle untill it glistened in the sun.
    A — B — C — D — E

27. Jenny liked to push her tongue against her tooth and make it woble like a rocking horse.
    A — B — C — D — E

28. The signed football was Fatima's favourite possession and she didn't want to loose it.
    A — B — C — D — E

29. The puppys were adorable, but Sam knew he would not be allowed to keep one.
    A — B — C — D — E

30. Harry liked hiding in the cupboard under the stares when he played hide and seek.
    A — B — C — D — E

/ 5

Total / 30

End of Test

Assessment Test 6

Allow 30 minutes to do this test and work as quickly and as carefully as you can.

You can print **multiple-choice answer sheets** for these questions from our website — go to cgpbooks.co.uk/11plus/answer-sheets or scan the QR code on the right. If you'd prefer to answer the questions on the page, just follow the instructions in the question.

Read this passage carefully and answer the questions that follow.

Aunt Florence

Some people thought that Ruby's aunt was slightly odd. Aunt Florence wore multi-coloured clothes, dyed her long hair as red as a post box and had peculiar habits (singing in the supermarket was a particularly embarrassing one). Ruby's older brother Alfie said that she got confused about what was real and what was imaginary.
5   Alfie said that this was because Aunt Florence was a writer, but Ruby believed everything she said.
    The day before yesterday, Aunt Flo had given Ruby a key: a thick, rusty, unimpressive-looking key. It looked as if it had not turned a lock in a long, long time, Ruby thought. Lowering her voice, Aunt Flo had told Ruby that it opened a
10 secret door in the attic of Grandpa's house; a door which led to another world. This was an enchanted world of magical people and strange creatures; a world Flo herself had visited when she was Ruby's age.
    "The door will only reveal itself," Ruby's aunt had whispered, "if the person holding the key believes that the magical door exists."
15 Now Ruby was standing alone in the dusty, disorderly, dimly-lit attic, holding the key. Grandpa's old train set was laid out in the middle of the floor, as if he had just been playing with it. Around the train set were boxes and books and old photo albums, all piled high. But there was no sign of a door.
    "Where are you? I know you are here, somewhere," Ruby said quietly as she
20 searched the room.
    Suddenly, the walls began to shake. Mortar crumbled from between the bricks and spiders scurried away from their cobwebs. Ruby stared in astonishment as a wonky, wooden door slowly appeared in the wall.

Answer these questions about the text that you've just read.
Circle the letter that matches the correct answer.

1. Which statement about Aunt Florence is not true?
   A   She has a niece and a nephew.
   B   She wears colourful clothes.
   C   She has strange habits.
   D   She has short hair.
   E   She sings in public.

2. When did Aunt Florence give Ruby the key?
   A   Two days ago
   B   One week ago
   C   One day ago
   D   Two weeks ago
   E   Three days ago

3. How did Aunt Florence speak to Ruby when she gave her the key?
   A   Quickly
   B   Loudly
   C   Quietly
   D   Angrily
   E   Jokingly

4. How did Aunt Florence know about the door?
   A   She had gone through it a few days ago.
   B   Grandpa had told her about it last year.
   C   Her older brother had told her about it.
   D   She had written about it in one of her books.
   E   She had gone through it when she was younger.

5. Which of the following statements about the attic is not true?
   A   It was untidy.
   B   It was dark.
   C   It was dirty.
   D   It was in Aunt Florence's house.
   E   It was filled with boxes and other old things.

/ 5

Assessment Test 6

Answer these questions about the text that you've just read.
Circle the letter that matches the correct answer.

6. What does Ruby have to do to reveal the door to the enchanted world?

   A Tell the door to reveal itself.
   B Turn the key clockwise in the keyhole.
   C Believe that the door exists.
   D Rub the key until it shines.
   E Tap the wall three times.

7. Why did Ruby look at the door "in astonishment" (line 22)?

   A The door was made of gold.
   B The door was covered in cobwebs.
   C The door was breaking apart.
   D The door was open.
   E The door had appeared from nowhere.

/ 2

Answer these questions about the way words and phrases are used in the passage.

8. The word "imaginary" (line 4) could most accurately be replaced by:

   A factual.
   B dishonest.
   C honest.
   D invented.
   E copied.

9. Which of these words is closest in meaning to "reveal" (line 13)?

   A Find
   B Unlock
   C Show
   D Open
   E Hide

10. Which of these words is closest in meaning to the word "unimpressive" (line 8)?

    A Ordinary
    B Unusual
    C Unclear
    D Rare
    E Amazing

/ 3

Carry on to the next question → →

Assessment Test 6

Answer these questions about the way words and phrases are used in the passage.

11. "Ruby said quietly as she searched the room" (lines 19-20).
    Which of these words is an adverb?

    A Ruby
    B said
    C quietly
    D searched
    E room

12. "dusty, disorderly, dimly-lit" (line 15). This is an example of:

    A a rhyme.
    B alliteration.
    C a simile.
    D a metaphor.
    E onomatopoeia.

/ 2

In each sentence, there is one punctuation mistake. Circle the letter which matches the part of the sentence with the mistake.

13. There are free reading group's for children in the library every Saturday morning.
    | A | B | C | D | E |

14. Great-Grandma and her friends went on a coach trip to Milton Keynes for her Birthday.
    | A | B | C | D | E |

15. Remote-controlled battling robots are going to be one of the top-selling toys this year?
    | A | B | C | D | E |

16. Holidays are a time to relax, play, try new activities, and spend time with family.
    | A | B | C | D | E |

17. Is the new sports centre going to open to the public in the summer or autumn!
    | A | B | C | D | E |

18. It was Lord Freds job to defend his castle, battle evil armies and to fight for the king.
    | A | B | C | D | E |

19. "Help me, please help! screeched the baker, as a cheeky mouse scurried across the floor.
    | A | B | C | D | E |

20. Its really important for your health to eat some fruit and vegetables every day.
    | A | B | C | D | E |

/ 8

Assessment Test 6

> In each sentence, there is one spelling mistake. Circle the letter which matches the part of the sentence with the mistake.

21. Amber handed out loads of copys of her flyer on how to recycle household rubbish.
    A   B   C   D   E

22. As a spesial favour to his dad, Matthew took his sister to the optician on Monday.
    A   B   C   D   E

23. Holly peared through the gaps between the shrubs and trees, looking for her dog.
    A   B   C   D   E

24. Ibrahim worked hard in his gitar lessons so that he would be ready for the concert.
    A   B   C   D   E

25. Laila needed help because the knot in the skipping rope was tide so tightly.
    A   B   C   D   E

/ 5

> Choose the right word or phrase to fill the gap.
> Circle the letter which matches the correct word.

26. Yesterday I had to go to the dentist and I **aren't hadn't weren't isn't wasn't**
                                                  A   B   C   D   E

27. looking forward to it. However, **if when but how on** I got there, the dentist
                                       A   B   C   D   E

28. **looks seen looked look saw** at my teeth and said that they were the best teeth
        A   B   C   D   E

29. she **had have hadn't has hasn't** seen all week. Then she gave me a sticker
          A   B   C   D   E

30. and **said tells tell told says** me to keep up the good work.
           A   B   C   D   E

/ 5

Total / 30

End of Test

Assessment Test 6

Assessment Test 7

Allow 30 minutes to do this test and work as quickly and as carefully as you can.

You can print **multiple-choice answer sheets** for these questions from our website — go to cgpbooks.co.uk/11plus/answer-sheets or scan the QR code on the right. If you'd prefer to answer the questions on the page, just follow the instructions in the question.

Read this passage carefully and answer the questions that follow.

The Ancient Olympics

The first Olympic Games were held nearly 3000 years ago in Greece. They were held to honour Zeus, king of the gods, and took place in a stadium in the valley of Olympia. The Olympics were celebrated every four years as a sporting and religious festival and could draw large crowds of up to 40,000 people.

5   The games started with worship in a great temple near the stadium. A specially carved statue of Zeus made from gold and ivory, six times bigger than the average man, was the focus of the celebrations. The competitors had to swear an oath* to Zeus that they had trained for ten months to prepare for the events.

After the ceremony, the games began. One of the most demanding events was
10 the pentathlon. This consisted of five activities: running, throwing the javelin (a spear), throwing a discus (a metal disc), wrestling and long jump, and required great strength and determination from the athletes. The final race of the games was the challenging hoplite race, where the runners had to wear armour and carry shields. The winner of each Olympic event was presented with a special crown made from
15 olive leaves.

The Olympic Games were held for over a thousand years until they were banned by the Romans. They were restarted as the modern Olympics in 1896. The modern games include many of the same events as the ancient games, such as races and the long jump, as well as new activities like swimming and fencing. Although the
20 Olympics are now held all over the world, they are still celebrated every four years.

*oath — *promise*

Answer these questions about the text that you've just read.
Circle the letter that matches the correct answer.

1. Where did the sporting events of the Ancient Olympics take place?

    A   In the great temple
    B   In a stadium in Olympia
    C   In a different district every four years
    D   In stadiums all over the world
    E   In the mountains of Greece

2. For how long were the Ancient Olympics held before being banned?

    A   40,000 years
    B   more than 3000 years
    C   more than 1000 years
    D   1896 years
    E   less than 4 years

3. What did the winners receive?

    A   Gold and ivory
    B   A specially carved statue of Zeus
    C   A medal
    D   A chariot
    E   A crown made of leaves

4. According to the text, which of the following statements about Zeus is not true?

    A   Zeus was king of the gods.
    B   The games ended with everybody worshipping Zeus.
    C   The statue of Zeus was taller than a man.
    D   All the athletes made a promise to Zeus.
    E   The Olympic Games were held to honour Zeus.

5. Why was the hoplite race difficult?

    A   It was the final race of the games.
    B   It was the last event in the pentathlon.
    C   The runners had travelled from all over Greece.
    D   The runners had to run long distances.
    E   The runners had to wear heavy armour.

/ 5

Carry on to the next question → →

Assessment Test 7

> Answer these questions about the text that you've just read.
> Circle the letter that matches the correct answer.

6. Which of the following does not describe the Ancient Olympic Games?

    A It was a sporting festival.
    B It was held to honour Zeus.
    C It could draw large crowds of thousands of people.
    D It was dedicated to the king of the Greeks.
    E It was a religious festival.

7. Which of the following words describes the statue of Zeus?

    A Ugly
    B Shabby
    C Impressive
    D Ignored
    E Small

/ 2

> Answer these questions about the way words and phrases are used in the passage.

8. Which of these phrases means the same as "to honour Zeus" (line 2)?

    A To crown Zeus
    B To ask Zeus for a favour
    C To visit Zeus
    D To vote for Zeus
    E To praise Zeus

9. Which of these words is closest in meaning to "competitors" (line 7)?

    A Contestants
    B Men
    C Priests
    D People
    E Audience

10. Which of these words could most accurately replace "strength" (line 12)?

    A Power
    B Muscles
    C Training
    D Skill
    E Size

/ 3

Assessment Test 7

Answer these questions about the way words and phrases are used in the passage.

11. "great" (line 5) and "special" (line 14) are examples of which part of speech?

    A Nouns
    B Verbs
    C Adverbs
    D Adjectives
    E Pronouns

12. "The modern games include many of the same events" (lines 17-18). Which of these words is a verb?

    A modern
    B games
    C include
    D many
    E same

/ 2

In each sentence, there is one spelling mistake. Circle the letter which matches the part of the sentence with the mistake.

13. Dangerus materials, such as fireworks, must be kept away from children for their safety.
    A   B   C   D   E

14. The audition was really tuff, but Georgina knew she had done her best when it was over.
    A   B   C   D   E

15. The hairy monkies at the zoo were wonderful and sent Dad rushing for his camera.
    A   B   C   D   E

16. Jokeingly, Grandpa placed a rubber spider and a rotten egg in Mum's wellington boot.
    A   B   C   D   E

17. The pirates swore they never toucht the captain's chocolate, but the parrot disagreed.
    A   B   C   D   E

18. The princess hated being throne over people's shoulders when they rescued her.
    A   B   C   D   E

19. The vampire had a memerable visit to the dentist's and said she'd never visit him again.
    A   B   C   D   E

20. The waiter brought knifes, forks, spoons and glasses to the table, but forgot the food.
    A   B   C   D   E

/ 8

Carry on to the next question → →

Choose the right word or phrase to fill the gap.
Circle the letter which matches the correct word.

21. The netball team are celebrating **some an lots many one** great news.
                                                            A   B   C   D   E

22. They have **lifted went beaten left won** the finals of the national championships!
                         A   B   C   D   E

23. At first, they **made make may makes maid** us all believe that they
                        A   B   C   D   E

24. **have did has had would** lost. We knew they were tricking us though, because
       A   B   C   D   E

25. they couldn't stop smiling! There **is will was were have** be a party to celebrate.
                                                       A   B   C   D   E

/ 5

In each sentence, there is one punctuation mistake. Circle the letter which matches the part of the sentence with the mistake.

26. The umpire said that the batsman was out, even though he hadnt touched the ball.
         A   B   C   D   E

27. As she polished the car, Razia hoped that her dad would let her go to the park".
         A   B   C   D   E

28. Although she was only six, Lynn loved reading books' about racing motorbikes.
         A   B   C   D   E

29. Alex found that planting Trees for the new woodland by the river was fun and rewarding.
         A   B   C   D   E

30. Amir went on the carousel, the spinning teacups the dodgems and the big wheel.
         A   B   C   D   E

/ 5

Total   / 30

End of Test

Assessment Test 7

Assessment Test 8

Allow 30 minutes to do this test and work as quickly and as carefully as you can.

You can print **multiple-choice answer sheets** for these questions from our website — go to cgpbooks.co.uk/11plus/answer-sheets or scan the QR code on the right. If you'd prefer to answer the questions on the page, just follow the instructions in the question.

Read this poem carefully and answer the questions that follow.

Winter Time

Late lies the wintry sun a-bed,
A frosty, fiery sleepy-head;
Blinks but an hour or two; and then,
A blood-red orange, sets again.

5 Before the stars have left the skies,
At morning in the dark I rise;
And shivering in my nakedness,
By the cold candle, bathe and dress.

Close by the jolly fire I sit
10 To warm my frozen bones a bit;
Or with a reindeer-sled, explore
The colder countries round the door.

When to go out, my nurse doth wrap
Me in my comforter* and cap;
15 The cold wind burns my face, and blows
Its frosty pepper up my nose.

Black are my steps on silver sod**;
Thick blows my frosty breath abroad;
And tree and house, and hill and lake,
20 Are frosted like a wedding-cake.

by Robert Louis Stevenson

*comforter — *a scarf*
**sod — *soil*

Answer these questions about the text that you've just read.
Circle the letter that matches the correct answer.

1. Which of these things is not mentioned in the poem?
   - **A** Sun
   - **B** Fire
   - **C** Candle
   - **D** Stars
   - **E** Moon

2. What does the nurse do?
   - **A** Make clothes for the child.
   - **B** Put the child to bed.
   - **C** Dress the child.
   - **D** Wake the child up.
   - **E** Take the child out to play.

3. Why does the child dress by candlelight?
   - **A** The child is cold.
   - **B** It is night time.
   - **C** It is dark in the morning.
   - **D** The child doesn't want to wake anyone else.
   - **E** The child is scared of the dark.

4. What happens in lines 15-16?
   - **A** The wind has black specks in it.
   - **B** The wind is so hot that it burns the child's face.
   - **C** Somebody spills pepper.
   - **D** The wind is so cold that it stings the child's face.
   - **E** The child can't stop sneezing.

5. Which of these events happens last in the poem?
   - **A** The child goes outside.
   - **B** The child gets up in the dark.
   - **C** The child shivers in the candlelight.
   - **D** The child washes and gets dressed.
   - **E** The child gets warm by the fire.

/ 5

Assessment Test 8

Answer these questions about the text that you've just read.
Circle the letter that matches the correct answer.

6. What is the first verse about?

   A The stars twinkling in the sky.
   B The sun melting the snow.
   C The sun rising and setting.
   D The child getting up late.
   E The child playing in the sun.

7. In line 17, the child notices that the frost is melted by:

   A the rain.
   B pepper.
   C the fire.
   D the reindeer sled.
   E footsteps.

/ 2

Answer these questions about the way words and phrases are used in the poem.

8. Which of these words is closest in meaning to "shivering" (line 7)?

   A Trembling
   B Sobbing
   C Heating
   D Hurting
   E Freezing

9. Which of these words is closest in meaning to "jolly" (line 9)?

   A Merry
   B Friendly
   C Warm
   D Excited
   E Funny

10. Which of the following is closest in meaning to "explore" (line 11)?

    A Move from
    B Travel around
    C Arrive
    D Depart from
    E Admire

/ 3

Carry on to the next question →→

Assessment Test 8

68

> Answer these questions about the way words and phrases are used in the poem.

11. "To warm my frozen bones a bit" (line 10). Which of these words is an adjective?

    A warm
    B my
    C frozen
    D bones
    E bit

12. "hill and lake, / Are frosted like a wedding-cake." (lines 19-20). This is an example of:

    A a metaphor.
    B a simile.
    C a question.
    D an apostrophe.
    E an exclamation.

/ 2

> In each sentence, there is one punctuation mistake. Circle the letter which matches the part of the sentence with the mistake.

13. Rose was hoping to invite Josh, Sven Paula and Andy to the evening football match.
    A   B   C   D   E

14. Brian's children, Ana and Meg, were really looking forward to their holiday in france.
    A   B   C   D   E

15. Mrs Jones was determined, to finish her novel and worked hard on it every day.
    A   B   C   D   E

16. The tiger which looked as though it was asleep, suddenly jumped up with a roar!
    A   B   C   D   E

17. After walking on the moor, Phil's shoes were covered in thick, mud, grass and leaves.
    A   B   C   D   E

18. The evil mouse threatened the terrified crowd, Give me all your cheese or else!"
    A   B   C   D   E

19. The ballet class are really excited because theyre going to London to see Swan Lake.
    A   B   C   D   E

20. Parvati hid behind a cushion and said, trembling, "This part of the film is really scary"!
    A   B   C   D   E

/ 8

Assessment Test 8

In each sentence, there is one spelling mistake. Circle the letter which matches the part of the sentence with the mistake.

21. The pilot landed / the plane safely / on the runway / during the / awfull storm.
    A / B / C / D / E

22. The cat was / a pityful sight / when she came / in looking like / a drowned rat.
    A / B / C / D / E

23. Many people / believe that / you will get seven years / bad luck if / you brake a mirror.
    A / B / C / D / E

24. Ice skating / is really fun / and has become / very populer / on outdoor rinks at Christmas.
    A / B / C / D / E

25. The duckling / waddled across / the garden, / draging a wiggling / worm along behind it.
    A / B / C / D / E

/ 5

Choose the right word or phrase to fill the gap. Circle the letter which matches the correct word.

26. Riding a unicycle requires an excellent sense **if about in to of** balance.
    A   B   C   D E

27. I **bought bring brought buy buyed** one from a junk shop last week and
    A   B   C   D   E

28. I've been practising in the park **away beside next in front between** our house.
    A   B   C   D   E

29. At first, I **wouldn't haven't mustn't couldn't shouldn't** even stay upright
    A   B   C   D   E

30. for two seconds, but now I can **rode riding ride rider rid** with my eyes closed!
    A   B   C   D   E

/ 5

Total / 30

End of Test

Assessment Test 8

Glossary

adjective	A word that describes a noun, e.g. "sunny morning", "frosty lawn".
adverb	A word that describes a verb, e.g. "She sang loudly."
alliteration	The repetition of a sound at the beginning of words within a phrase, e.g. "Loopy Lois likes lipstick."
antonym	A word with the opposite meaning to another word, e.g. "on" and "off".
collective noun	A name for a group of things, e.g. "a flock of sheep".
fiction	Text that has been made up by the author, about imaginary people and events.
homophones	Words that sound the same, but mean different things, e.g. "hair" and "hare".
imagery	Language that creates a vivid picture in the reader's mind.
metaphor	A way of describing something by saying that it is something else, e.g. "Mr Smith was an angry dragon."
non-fiction	Text that is about facts and real people and events.
noun	A word that names something, e.g. "scissors", "chair".
onomatopoeia	When words sound like the noise they describe, e.g. "pop", "bang".
phrase	A part of a sentence without a verb which doesn't make sense on its own, e.g. "the purple dress".
plural	More than one of something, e.g. "birds".
prefix	A letter or letters that can be added to the start of a word to change its meaning, e.g. "unlock".
pronoun	Words that can be used instead of nouns, e.g. "I", "you", "he", "it".
proper noun	A name for a particular place, thing or person, e.g. "James", "Paris".
simile	A way of describing something by comparing it to something else, e.g. "The stars were like a thousand diamonds."
suffix	A letter or letters that can be added to the end of a word to change its meaning, e.g. "useful".
synonym	A word with a similar meaning to another word, e.g. "big" and "huge".
verb	An action or being word, e.g. "I run", "he went", "we think".

Answers

Page 2 — Parts Of Speech

1) **cat**
'cat' is a noun because it is the name of an animal.
2) **Margot**
'Margot' is a noun because it is the name of a person.
3) **her**
'her' is a pronoun because it takes the place of a noun in the sentence.
4) **pack**
'pack' is a collective noun because it is the name for a group of wolves.
5) **monster**
'monster' is a noun because it is the name of a creature.
6) **ours**
'ours' is a pronoun because it takes the place of a noun in the sentence.
7) **He**
'He' is a pronoun because it takes the place of a noun in the sentence.
8) **flock**
'flock' is a collective noun because it is the name for a group of birds.
9) **many answers possible**
Some ideas are 'the yellow bananas from Spain' or 'the ripe bananas in the fruit bowl'.
10) **many answers possible**
Some ideas are 'the old police officer in the car' or 'the brave police officer on the street'.
11) **many answers possible**
Some ideas are 'the clean lion near the bath' or 'the fearsome lion with sharp teeth'.

Page 3 — Parts Of Speech

1) **famous**
'famous' is an adjective because it describes the noun in the sentence — 'explorer'.
2) **quickly**
'quickly' is an adverb because it describes the verb — 'sprinted'.
3) **professional**
'professional' is an adjective because it describes the noun in the sentence — 'chef'.
4) **funny**
'funny' is an adjective because it describes the noun — 'clown'.
5) **desperately**
'desperately' is an adverb because it describes the verb phrase — 'was trying'.
6) **important**
'important' is an adjective because it describes the noun — 'instructions'.
7) **confidently**
'confidently' is an adverb because it describes the verb — 'walked'.
8) **gracefully**
'gracefully' is the best adverb here because it means 'showing beauty of movement'.
9) **swiftly**
'swiftly' is the best adverb here because it means 'quickly'.
10) **cheerfully**
'cheerfully' is the best adverb here because it means 'happily'.
11) **closely**
'closely' is the best adverb here because it means 'near' in terms of the relationship between lions and leopards.
12) **obediently**
'obediently' is the best adverb here because it means 'in a well-behaved manner'.
13) **boldly**
'boldly' is the best adverb here because it means 'bravely and with confidence'.
14) **faintly**
'faintly' is the best adverb here because it means 'slightly'.

Page 4 — Verbs

1) **went**
'went' is the verb because it is the action word in the sentence.
2) **loves**
'loves' is the verb because it is the action word in the sentence.
3) **bought**
'bought' is the verb because it is the action word in the sentence.
4) **danced**
'danced' is the verb because it is the action word in the sentence.
5) **took**
'took' is the verb because it is the action word in the sentence.
6) **snored**
'snored' is the verb because it is the action word in the sentence.
7) **shut**
'shut' is the verb because it is the action word in this sentence.
8) **sang**
'sang' is the correct verb because the sentence is in the past tense.
9) **escaped**
'escaped' is the correct verb because the sentence is in the past tense.
10) **ate**
'ate' is the correct verb because the sentence is in the past tense.
11) **want**
'want' is the correct verb because the sentence is in the present tense.
12) **kept**
'kept' is the correct verb because the sentence is in the past tense.
13) **hung**
'hung' is the correct verb because the sentence is in the past tense.
14) **had**
'had' is the correct verb because the sentence is in the past tense.

Page 5 — Verbs

1) **raced**
The sentence should be 'Minna ran away from the dog that raced towards her.' This is the correct past tense form of the verb 'to race'.
2) **looked**
The sentence should be 'Wen looked around the carriage for his dad.' This is the correct past tense form of the verb 'to look'.
3) **brought**
The sentence should be 'Fin brought his colouring pencils to the art class.' This is the correct past tense form of the verb 'to bring'.
4) **took**
The sentence should be 'Henry took the bus to work on Wednesday.' This is the correct past tense form of the verb 'to take'.
5) **ate**
The sentence should be 'Paula had made a picnic which they ate in the park.' This is the correct past tense form of the verb 'to eat'.

6) made
The sentence should be 'Mary joined the knitting club and made a scarf.' This is the correct past tense form of the verb 'to make'.

7) thought
The sentence should be 'Gary thought that the Brussels sprouts tasted awful.' This is the correct past tense form of the verb 'to think'.

8) claps
The sentence should be 'Ibrahim claps to celebrate the victory.' This is the correct present tense form of the verb 'to clap' and agrees with the noun — 'Ibrahim'.

9) wishes
The sentence should be 'Mette wishes that she could wear trousers to school.' This is the correct present tense form of the verb 'to wish' and agrees with the noun — 'Mette'.

10) wobbles
The sentence should be 'The orange jelly wobbles gently on the tray.' This is the correct present tense form of the verb 'to wobble' and agrees with the noun — 'jelly'.

11) chooses
The sentence should be 'Leon chooses to join the orchestra.' This is the correct present tense form of the verb 'to choose' and agrees with the noun — 'Leon'.

12) leaves
The sentence should be 'Hannah leaves the building by the back staircase'. This is the correct present tense form of the verb 'to leave' and agrees with the noun — 'Hannah'.

13) blow
The sentence should be 'I blow a huge bubble in the bright sunlight.' This is the correct present tense form of the verb 'to blow' and agrees with the pronoun — 'I'.

14) buys
The sentence should be 'Maria buys the tartan trousers.' This is the correct present tense form of the verb 'to buy' and agrees with the noun — 'Maria'.

Page 6 — Mixed Grammar Questions

1) orange
'orange' is the adjective in this sentence.

2) Mary
'Mary' is the proper noun in this sentence.

3) loudly
'loudly' is the adverb in this sentence.

4) favourite
'favourite' is the adjective in this sentence.

5) patiently
'patiently' is the adverb in this sentence.

6) landed
'landed' is the verb in this sentence.

7) marathon
'marathon' is the common noun in this sentence.

8) mine
'mine' is the pronoun in this sentence.

9) sparkled
'sparkled' is the verb in this sentence.

10) frightened
'frightened' is the adjective in this sentence.

11) already
'already' is the adverb in this sentence.

12) him
'him' is the pronoun in this sentence.

13) older
'older' is the adjective in this sentence.

14) piano
'piano' is the common noun in this sentence.

15) blew
'blew' is the verb in this sentence.

Page 7 — Mixed Grammar Questions

1) worked
The sentence should be 'We worked really hard to win the dance competition.' This is the correct past tense form of the verb 'to work' and agrees with the pronoun — 'We'.

2) tore
The sentence should be 'The certificate tore in half when they both grabbed it.' This is the correct past tense form of the verb 'to tear' and agrees with the noun — 'certificate'.

3) watching
The sentence should be 'Milena was watching the TV when her brother arrived.' This is correct because it shows what Milena was doing when her brother arrived and it completes the phrase 'Milena was watching'.

4) caring
The sentence should be 'The nurse is caring for his patients.' This is correct because it shows what the nurse is doing and it completes the phrase 'the nurse is caring'.

5) kindly
The sentence should be 'Dad kindly offered to drive us home after the party.' 'kindly' is the correct word because it is an adverb which describes the verb 'offered'.

6) you
The sentence should be 'Tola is going to meet you at the bus station.' 'you' is the correct word because the others are possessive pronouns.

7) threw
The sentence should be 'Gus threw the cricket ball the furthest at last year's sports day.' This is the correct past tense form of the verb 'to throw'.

8) flock
The sentence should be 'The flock of sheep was in the middle of the road.' This is the correct collective noun for a group of sheep.

9) shining
The sentence should be 'The sun was shining through the gap in the blinds.' This is correct because it shows what the sun was doing and it completes the phrase 'the sun was shining'.

10) his
The sentence should be 'Henry's trip to France was his first holiday abroad.' This is the correct pronoun to go with the noun 'Henry'.

11) bravery
The sentence should be 'Ava showed great bravery by rescuing the cat from the tree.' 'bravery' is correct because it is a noun which agrees with the adjective 'great' to form the phrase 'great bravery'.

12) run
The sentence should be 'Nena had run around the park in the morning before work.' This is correct because it is the only option which makes sense and it completes the phrase 'Nena had run'.

13) softly
The sentence should be 'Geoff whistled softly as he cleaned the car.' 'softly' is the correct word because it is an adverb which describes the verb — 'whistled'.

14) had
The sentence should be 'My sister had brown hair before she dyed it purple.' This is the correct past tense form of the verb — 'to have'.

15) lit
The sentence should be 'Beth lit the candles in the sitting room yesterday.' This is the correct past tense form of the verb — 'to light'.

Answers

Page 8 — Starting And Ending Sentences

1) ?
This is a question so it needs a question mark.
2) ?
This is a question so it needs a question mark.
3) !
This shows strong feelings so it needs an exclamation mark.
4) !
This shows strong feelings so it needs an exclamation mark.
5) ?
This is a question so it needs a question mark.
6) <u>C</u>an you go in the car with Suki<u>?</u> <u>W</u>e'll phone you when we arrive<u>.</u>
You get one mark for a capital letter at the start of 'Can', one mark for a question mark after 'Suki', one mark for a capital letter at the start of 'We'll' and one mark for a full stop at the end of 'arrive'.
7) <u>M</u>y dad has been bald for years<u>.</u> Luckily, the hairdresser polishes his head for free<u>.</u>
You get one mark for a capital letter at the start of 'My', one mark for a full stop at the end of 'years', one mark for a capital letter at the start of 'Luckily' and one mark for a full stop at the end of 'free'.
8) <u>W</u>e're having an Easter egg hunt in the garden<u>.</u> <u>W</u>hat time should it start<u>?</u>
You get one mark for a capital letter at the start of 'We're', one mark for a full stop at the end of 'garden', one mark for a capital letter at the start of 'What' and one mark for a question mark at the end of 'start'.

Page 9 — Commas

1) been, in
The comma between 'been' and 'in' should be circled.
2) room, fills
The comma between 'room' and 'fills' should be circled.
3) and, heavy
The comma between 'and' and 'heavy' should be circled.
4) up, some
The comma between 'up' and 'some' should be circled.
5) wait, until
The comma between 'wait' and 'until' should be circled.
6) rocks, on
The comma between 'rocks' and 'on' should be circled.
7) stone, lighthouse
The comma between 'stone' and 'lighthouse' should be circled.
8) dinner, I
The sentence should be 'Before <u>dinner, I</u> practised playing the accordion.'
9) maze, Mum
The sentence should be 'As we entered the <u>maze, Mum</u> led the way towards the centre.'
10) fright, I
The sentence should be 'Because of my stage <u>fright, I</u> get nervous before our concerts.'
11) forecast, we
The sentence should be 'Despite the bad weather <u>forecast, we</u> took a risk and went for a walk.'
12) water, stir
The sentence should be 'Once you've mixed in the <u>water, stir</u> the dough for five minutes.'
13) summer, the
The sentence should be 'Even during the <u>summer, the</u> rooms in the castle remain cool.'
14) painting, don't
The sentence should be 'After you've finished <u>painting, don't</u> forget to clean your brushes.'

Page 10 — Apostrophes

1) Will's
'Will's' is correct here — the apostrophe shows that the dog belongs to 'Will' and 'Will' is singular so the apostrophe should go before the 's'.
2) woman's
'woman's' is correct here — the apostrophe shows that the goat belongs to the woman. 'woman' is the singular form of the noun so the apostrophe goes before the 's'.
3) bird's
'bird's' is correct here — the apostrophe shows that the wing belongs to the bird. There is only one bird, so the apostrophe goes before the 's'.
4) men's
'men's' is correct here — the apostrophe shows that the children belong to the men. 'men' is already a plural noun so the apostrophe goes before the 's'.
5) players'
'players'' is correct here — the apostrophe shows that the lunches belong to the players. 'players' is plural and ends in 's' so the apostrophe goes after the 's'.
6) Marc's pets
The apostrophe shows that the pets belong to Marc and Marc is singular so the apostrophe goes before the 's'.
7) the boys' water
The apostrophe shows that the water belongs to the boys. 'boys' is plural and ends in 's' so the apostrophe goes after the 's'.
8) the girl's gloves
The apostrophe shows that the gloves belong to the girl. There is only one girl so the apostrophe goes before the 's'.
9) the wolves' paws
The apostrophe shows that the paws belong to the wolves. 'wolves' is plural and ends in 's' so the apostrophe goes after the 's'.
10) the women's mugs
The apostrophe shows that the mugs belong to the women. 'women' is already plural so the apostrophe goes before the 's'.

Page 11 — Apostrophes

1) can't
'cannot' becomes 'can't' — the apostrophe replaces the missing 'n' and 'o'.
2) you've
'you have' becomes 'you've' — the apostrophe replaces the missing 'h' and 'a'.
3) I'd
'I would' becomes 'I'd' — the apostrophe replaces the missing 'w', 'o', 'u' and 'l'.
4) They're
'They are' becomes 'They're' — the apostrophe replaces the missing 'a'.
5) We're
'We are' becomes 'We're' — the apostrophe replaces the missing 'a'.
6) wasn't
'was not' becomes 'wasn't' — the apostrophe replaces the missing 'o'.
7) shouldn't
'should not' becomes 'shouldn't' — the apostrophe replaces the missing 'o'.
8) its
'its' shows that the lead belongs to the dog so it doesn't need an apostrophe.
9) it's
'it's' is a shortened version of 'it has' so it needs an apostrophe.
10) its
'its' shows that the toy mouse belongs to the cat so it doesn't need an apostrophe.

11) its
'its' shows that the uniform policy belongs to the school so it doesn't need an apostrophe.
12) It's
'It's' is a shortened version of 'it has' so it needs an apostrophe.
13) its
'its' shows that the stall belongs to the café so it doesn't need an apostrophe.
14) it's
'it's' is a shortened version of 'it is' so it needs an apostrophe.

Page 12 — Inverted Commas

1) I really want a pirate costume,
The words that are spoken are inside the inverted commas.
2) Look Gary, carrots are on offer,
The words that are spoken are inside the inverted commas.
3) Get down off that wall!
The words that are spoken are inside the inverted commas.
4) How long will the roadworks go on for?
The words that are spoken are inside the inverted commas.
5) I'll have the tomato salad, please,
The words that are spoken are inside the inverted commas.
6) How did you get here?
The words that are spoken are inside the inverted commas.
7) Look! There's a gorilla in the bath!
The words that are spoken are inside the inverted commas.
8) "It's a long shot," said Pete.
The inverted commas go around the words that are spoken — the second pair need to go after the comma.
9) "There must be a way to escape," she whispered.
The inverted commas go around the words that are spoken — the second pair need to go after the comma.
10) Basha complained, "I don't want to play cricket."
The inverted commas go around the words that are spoken — the second pair need to go after the full stop.
11) "Jump!" shouted Harish to the lady at the window.
The inverted commas go around the words that are spoken — the second pair need to go after the exclamation mark.
12) "I don't believe you," said Miranda.
The inverted commas go around the words that are spoken — the second pair need to go after the comma.
13) The giant growled, "Where's that child?"
The inverted commas go around the words that are spoken — the second pair need to go after the question mark.
14) We all cheered, "Come on Red Team!"
The inverted commas go around the words that are spoken — the second pair need to go after the exclamation mark.

Page 13 — Inverted Commas

1) "My guinea pig ate my homework," said Arusha.
There should be a comma at the end of the speech and a full stop at the end of the sentence.
2) Mum asked, "How did you get so filthy?"
There should be a comma before the speech starts and a question mark before the second pair of inverted commas.
3) Sheila muttered, "Why can't you be on time?"
There should be a comma before the speech starts and a question mark before the second pair of inverted commas.
4) "I got lost on Frencham Street," I explained.
There should be a comma before the second pair of inverted commas and a full stop at the end of the sentence.

5) Tim whined, "You're hogging the best skateboard."
There should be a comma before the speech starts and a full stop before the second pair of inverted commas.
6) "My lucky socks have spaceships on them," said Caleb.
There should be a comma before the second pair of inverted commas and a full stop at the end of the sentence.
7) Lena whispered, "He didn't know that."
There is one mark for each piece of punctuation added: inverted commas go before and after the words that are spoken; there should be a comma before the speech starts; there should be a capital letter at the start of the speech; and there should be a full stop at the end of the speech, before the second pair of inverted commas.
8) Amit declared, "That's Joey's little black dog."
There is one mark for each piece of punctuation added: inverted commas go before and after the words that are spoken; there should be a comma before the speech starts; there should be a capital letter at the start of the speech; and there should be a full stop at the end of the speech, before the second pair of inverted commas.
9) Osei asked, "Where has she hidden our presents?"
There is one mark for each piece of punctuation added: inverted commas go before and after the words that are spoken; there should be a comma before the speech starts; there should be a capital letter at the start of the speech; and there should be a question mark at the end of the speech, before the second pair of inverted commas.
10) "Everyone stop right now!" Martia shouted.
There is one mark for each piece of punctuation added: inverted commas go either side of the words that are spoken; there should be a capital letter at the start of the speech; there should be an exclamation mark at the end of the speech, before the second pair of inverted commas; and there should be a full stop at the end of the sentence.

Page 14 — Mixed Punctuation Questions

1) cellar!".
The sentence should be '"We've got to get out of the cellar!"' There shouldn't be a full stop after the inverted commas.
2) house, has
The sentence should be 'Our house has six floors, twelve bedrooms and a cinema.' There shouldn't be a comma between 'house' and 'has'.
3) Charlie's
The sentence should be 'Can we swim when we get back from Charlie's house?' Proper nouns should start with a capital letter.
4) talking,", said
The sentence should be '"I told you to stop talking," said Mrs Wu fiercely.' There shouldn't be a comma after the second pair of inverted commas.
5) Pink
The sentence should be 'The monster had ten legs, blue hair and a pink tail.' 'Pink' doesn't need a capital letter because it's not a proper noun and it's in the middle of a sentence.
6) My friend is moving to the Moon.
'My' should have a capital letter because it is at the beginning of the sentence.
7) Sophie's car had broken down.
The apostrophe in 'Sophie's' should go before the 's' because 'Sophie' is a singular noun.
8) Simon was looking forward to a holiday.
There should be a full stop at the end of the sentence.
9) "Where are the goats?" asked Jasminder.
There should be a second pair of inverted commas after the question mark.

10) "You're the only person who knows."
There should be an apostrophe in 'You're' because it is a shortened version of 'You are'.

Page 15 — Mixed Punctuation Questions

1) sport, he
The sentence should be, 'Although tennis is Stephen's favourite sport, he also plays football.' There should be a comma between 'sport' and 'he' to separate the two parts of the sentence.

2) it's
The sentence should be, 'I'm glad it's Friday tomorrow as I can't wait for the weekend.' There should be an apostrophe in 'it's' because it is a shortened form of 'it is'.

3) says, "Always
The sentence should be, 'Hugh often says, "Always look on the bright side of life."' There should be a comma before the first pair of inverted commas.

4) Finally, it's
The sentence should be, 'Finally, it's time to present the prize for Best Film.' There should be a comma after 'Finally' to separate the two parts of the sentence.

5) school?
The sentence should be, 'Why can't we wear skis to school?' This is a question so there should be a question mark at the end of the sentence.

6) piano's
The sentence should be, 'My piano's pedals are going rusty.' There should be an apostrophe in 'piano's' to show the pedals belong to the piano.

7) "You've
The sentence should be, '"You've done so well and I'm really proud," said Grandad.' There should be a pair of inverted commas before 'You've' to mark the beginning of the speech.

8) speakers, a
The sentence should be, 'My new computer has speakers, a mouse and lots of games.' There should be a comma between 'speakers' and 'a' to separate the items in the list.

9) won!" said
The sentence should be, '"I can't believe I won!" said Chloe happily.' There should be a second pair of inverted commas after 'won!' to mark the end of the speech.

10) They're
The sentence should be, 'They're coming to visit next weekend.' There should be an apostrophe in 'They're' because it is the shortened form of 'They are'.

11) child, I
The sentence should be, 'Although I'm only a child, I like reading books about politics.' There should be a comma between 'child' and 'I' to separate the two parts of the sentence.

12) Sanctuary.
The sentence should be, 'The gala evening raised £2000 for Uppermill Donkey Sanctuary.' There should be a full stop at the end of the sentence.

13) hamsters, two
The sentence should be, 'Billy has three hamsters, two rabbits and a stick insect.' There should be a comma after 'hamsters' to separate the items in the list.

14) leaving? I
The sentence should be, '"When are we leaving? I don't want to be late."' There should be a question mark after 'leaving' because the speaker is asking a question.

15) lamb's
The sentence should be, 'The lamb's fleece was beautifully white in the sunshine.' There should be an apostrophe in 'lamb's' to show that the fleece belongs to the lamb.

Page 16 — Plurals

1) chefs
'chefs' is the correct plural — an 's' is added to 'chef'.

2) halves
'halves' is the correct plural — the 'f' is removed from 'half' and 'ves' is added.

3) wives
'wives' is the correct plural — the 'fe' is removed from 'wife' and 'ves' is added.

4) shelves
'shelves' is the correct plural — the 'f' is removed from 'shelf' and 'ves' is added.

5) safes
'safes' is the correct plural — an 's' is added to 'safe'.

6) beliefs
'beliefs' is the correct plural — an 's' is added to 'belief'.

7) lives
'lives' is the correct plural — the 'fe' is removed from 'life' and 'ves' is added.

8) fairies
'fairy' becomes 'fairies' — words ending in a consonant and a 'y' drop the 'y' and add 'ies' to make the plural.

9) boys
'boy' becomes 'boys' — words ending in a vowel and a 'y' add an 's' to make the plural.

10) days
'day' becomes 'days' — words ending in a vowel and a 'y' add an 's' to make the plural.

11) flies
'fly' becomes 'flies' — words ending in a consonant and a 'y' drop the 'y' and add 'ies' to make the plural.

12) hobbies
'hobby' becomes 'hobbies' — words ending in a consonant and a 'y' drop the 'y' and add 'ies' to make the plural.

13) ponies
'pony' becomes 'ponies' — words ending in a consonant and a 'y' drop the 'y' and add 'ies' to make the plural.

14) Daisies
'Daisy' becomes 'Daisies' — words ending in a consonant and a 'y' drop the 'y' and add 'ies' to make the plural.

Page 17 — Homophones

1) dear
'dear' makes sense here — it is an affectionate word used to describe a person, whereas a 'deer' is an animal.

2) grate
'grate' makes sense here — it is a word used in cooking, whereas 'great' means 'really good'.

3) bread
'bread' makes sense here — it is type of food, whereas 'bred' means 'produced children'.

4) would
'would' makes sense here — it completes the phrase, 'I would lend', whereas 'wood' is a material that comes from trees.

5) maid
'maid' makes sense here — it is a job, whereas 'made' means 'to produce'.

6) their
'their' makes sense here — it is a pronoun, whereas 'there' refers to a place.
7) seen
'seen' makes sense here — it is the past tense form of 'to see', whereas 'scene' refers to a place or setting.
8) to
'to' makes sense here — it shows the person's intentions.
9) two
'two' makes sense here — it is the word for the number 2.
10) too
'too' makes sense here — it means 'as well'.
11) to
'to' makes sense here — it completes the verb 'to unlock'.
12) too
'too' makes sense here — when added to 'much' it means 'an excessive amount'.
13) two
'two' makes sense here — it is the word for the number 2.
14) to
'to' makes sense here — it completes the verb 'to ride'.

Page 18 — Prefixes And Suffixes

1) disobedient
The correct prefix is 'dis'.
2) Reheat
The correct prefix is 'Re'.
3) unkind
The correct prefix is 'un'.
4) unusually
The correct prefix is 'un'.
5) nonsense
The correct prefix is 'non'.
6) impolite
The correct prefix is 'im'.
7) unable
The correct prefix is 'un'.
8) action
The correct suffix added is 'ion'.
9) collection
The correct suffix added is 'ion'.
10) similarity
The correct suffix added is 'ity'.
11) darkness
The correct suffix is 'ness'.
12) sadness
The correct suffix added is 'ness'.
13) navigation
The correct suffix is 'ion' — you need to remove the 'e' from 'navigate' before adding the suffix.
14) activity
The correct suffix is 'ity' — you need to remove the 'e' from 'active' before adding the suffix.

Page 19 — Awkward Spellings

1) a
The word is 'company'.
2) o
The word is 'factory'.

3) a
The word is 'miserable'.
4) e
The word is 'lottery'.
5) a
The word is 'calendar'.
6) e
The word is 'describe'.
7) i
The word is 'definitely'.
8) waded
The correct word is 'waded' — it has a single 'd' in the middle of the word.
9) tripped
The correct word is 'tripped' — it has a double 'p' in the middle of the word.
10) wrapping
The correct word is 'wrapping' — it has a double 'p' in the middle of the word.
11) chosen
The correct word is 'chosen' — it has a single 's' in the middle of the word.
12) robbed
The correct word is 'robbed' — it has a double 'b' in the middle of the word when it means 'stolen from'.
13) riding
The correct word is 'riding' — it has a single 'd' in the middle of the word when it means 'travelling on'.
14) thinner
The correct word is 'thinner' — it has a double 'n' in the middle of the word.

Page 20 — Mixed Spelling Questions

1) impatient
The correct prefix is 'im', not 'in'.
2) different
The correct suffix added to the root word 'differ' is 'ent', not 'ant'.
3) arches
'arch' becomes 'arches' — words ending in 'ch' add 'es' to make the plural.
4) tension
The correct ending is 'sion', not 'tion' — the root word is 'tense' so the 'e' is removed and 'ion' is added to make 'tension'.
5) Leaves
'Leaf' becomes 'Leaves' — often words ending in 'f' lose the 'f' and add 'ves' to make the plural.
6) blackberries
'blackberry' becomes 'blackberries' — words ending in a consonant and a 'y' drop the 'y' and add 'ies' to make the plural.
7) written
The correct word is 'written', not 'writen' — it has a double 't' in the middle of the word.
8) dishes
The correct word is 'dishes', not 'dishs' — words ending in 'sh' add 'es' to make the plural.
9) inactive
The correct prefix is 'in' not 'un'.
10) voluntary
The correct spelling of the word is 'voluntary', not 'voluntry' — an 'a' is needed.
11) stories
The correct spelling is 'stories' — words ending in a consonant and 'y' drop the 'y' and add 'ies' to make the plural.

12) **pinned**
The correct word is 'pinned', not 'pined' — the word means 'attached' so it should have a double 'n' in the middle of the word.

13) **pattern**
The correct word is 'pattern', not 'patern' — it has a double 't' in the middle of the word.

14) **purify**
The correct suffix is 'ify', not 'efy' — the root word is 'pure' and the 'e' is removed before the suffix is added.

15) **reference**
The correct suffix added to the root word 'refer' is 'ence', not 'ance'.

Page 21 — Mixed Spelling Questions

1) **smiling**
'smileing' is incorrect. You need to remove the 'e' before adding the suffix 'ing'.

2) **misread**
'missread' is incorrect. The prefix 'mis' only has one 's'.

3) **cliffs**
'cliffes' is incorrect. To make the plural of 'cliff' add 's'.

4) **coward**
'coword' is incorrect. The word ends in 'ard'.

5) **edible**
'edable' is incorrect. The word ends in 'ible'.

6) **important**
'inportant' is incorrect. The word begins in 'im'.

7) **favour**
'faver' is incorrect. The word ends in 'our'.

8) **watches**
'watchs' is incorrect. To make the plural of watch add 'es'.

9) **sunny**
'suny' is incorrect. There is a double 'n' in the middle of the word.

10) **their**
'there' is incorrect. 'their' and 'there' are homophones — 'their' is correct because it means 'belonging to them'.

11) **clothes**
'cloths' is incorrect. The word ends in 'es'.

12) **powerful**
'powerfull' is incorrect. The correct suffix is 'ful'.

13) **boundary**
'boundry' is incorrect. The word ends in 'ary'.

14) **tasteless**
'tastless' is incorrect. The letter 'e' at the end of 'taste' is not removed when the suffix 'less' is added.

15) **humming**
'huming' is incorrect. There is a double 'm' in the middle of the word.

Page 22 — Alliteration and Onomatopoeia

1) **many answers possible**
The 's' sound forms the alliteration. Some ideas are 'swing' or 'seesaw'.

2) **many answers possible**
The 't' sound forms the alliteration. Some ideas are 'terrific' or 'tangy'.

3) **many answers possible**
The 'p' sound forms the alliteration. Some ideas are 'pear' or 'peach'.

4) **many answers possible**
The 'ch' sound forms the alliteration. Some ideas are 'cheap' or 'cheesy'.

5) **many answers possible**
The 'w' sound forms the alliteration. Some ideas are 'white' or 'weird'.

6) **many answers possible**
The 'b' sound forms the alliteration. Some ideas are 'books' or 'boxing'.

7) **many answers possible**
The 's' sound forms the alliteration. Some ideas are 'sofa' or 'seat'.

8) **hooted**
'hooted' is onomatopoeic — it sounds like the noise an owl makes.

9) **crashed**
'crashed' is onomatopoeic — it sounds like the noise of someone moving loudly.

10) **grunt**
'grunt' is onomatopoeic — it sounds like the noise a pig makes.

11) **squelching**
'squelching' is onomatopoeic — it sounds like the noise you make when you walk through mud.

12) **clattered**
'clattered' is onomatopoeic — it sounds like the noise a metal object makes when it hits the floor.

13) **thud**
'thud' is onomatopoeic — it sounds like the noise of a heavy object hitting the floor.

14) **rattling**
'rattling' is onomatopoeic — it sounds like the noise a key would make in an old lock.

Page 23 — Imagery

1) **metaphor**
This is a metaphor because the football pitch is described as being a battlefield.

2) **metaphor**
This is a metaphor because the moon is described as being a white dinner plate in the sky.

3) **simile**
This is a simile because the fists are being compared to rocks.

4) **metaphor**
This is a metaphor because the brother is described as being an animal.

5) **metaphor**
This is a metaphor because the kitten is described as being a spoilt princess.

6) **simile**
This is a simile because the scarecrow is being compared to a statue.

7) **simile**
This is a simile because the eyes are being compared to diamonds.

8) **many answers possible**
The commonly used simile is 'as quiet as a <u>mouse</u>'.

9) **many answers possible**
The commonly used simile is 'as busy as a <u>bee</u>'.

10) **many answers possible**
The commonly used simile is 'as dry as a <u>bone</u>'.

11) **many answers possible**
The commonly used simile is 'as solid as a <u>rock</u>'.

12) **many answers possible**
The commonly used simile is 'as cold as <u>ice</u>'.

13) **many answers possible**
The commonly used simile is 'as light as a <u>feather</u>'.

14) **many answers possible**
The commonly used simile is 'as white as a <u>sheet</u>'.

Page 24 — Synonyms

1) **fix**
'fix' has the most similar meaning to 'mend'. They both mean 'to repair something'.
2) **happy**
'happy' has the most similar meaning to 'jolly'. They both mean 'joyful'.
3) **worried**
'worried' has the most similar meaning to 'concerned'. They both mean 'to feel anxious'.
4) **ocean**
'ocean' has the most similar meaning to 'sea'. They are both large bodies of salt water.
5) **intelligent**
'intelligent' has the most similar meaning to 'clever'. They both mean 'to show understanding and wisdom'.
6) **foolish**
'foolish' has the most similar meaning to 'silly'. They both mean 'unwise'.
7) **shiny**
'shiny' has the most similar meaning to 'glossy'. They both mean 'something that has a reflective surface'.
8) **sleepy**
'sleepy' has the most similar meaning to 'tired'. They both mean 'to feel weary'.
9) **running**
'running' has the most similar meaning to 'jogging'. They are both ways of travelling fast on foot.
10) **cabinet**
'cabinet' has the most similar meaning to 'cupboard'. They are both items of furniture used to store objects.
11) **kind**
'kind' has the most similar meaning to 'caring'. They both mean 'understanding and thoughtful'.
12) **leapt**
'leapt' has the most similar meaning to 'jumped'. They both mean 'to spring into the air'.
13) **viewed**
'viewed' has the most similar meaning to 'watched'. They both mean 'to look at something.'
14) **nervous**
'nervous' has the most similar meaning to 'uneasy'. They both mean 'to be concerned or worried'.

Page 25 — Antonyms

1) **wild**
'wild' has the opposite meaning to 'tame' — 'wild' means 'uncontrollable by humans', whereas 'tame' means 'under human control'.
2) **smiling**
'smiling' has the opposite meaning to 'frowning' — 'smiling' means 'having a happy facial expression', whereas 'frowning' means 'having a sad facial expression'.
3) **young**
'young' has the opposite meaning to 'elderly' — 'young' means 'someone who is not old', whereas 'elderly' means 'old'.
4) **distant**
'distant' has the opposite meaning to 'near' — 'distant' means 'far away', whereas 'near' means 'close by'.
5) **new**
'new' has the opposite meaning to 'old' — 'new' means 'something that has been made recently', whereas 'old' means 'something that has been around for a while'.
6) **healthy**
'healthy' has the opposite meaning to 'ill' — 'healthy' means 'in good health', whereas 'ill' means ' in poor health'.
7) **dirty**
'dirty' has the opposite meaning to 'clean' — 'dirty' means 'filthy', whereas 'clean' means 'not dirty'.
8) **hairy**
'hairy' has the opposite meaning to 'bald' — 'hairy' means 'with hair', whereas 'bald' means 'without hair'.
9) **late**
'late' has the opposite meaning to 'early' — 'late' means 'after a certain time', whereas 'early' means 'before a certain time'.
10) **praise**
'praise' has the opposite meaning to 'blame' — 'praise' means 'to say someone has done something well', whereas 'blame' means 'to say that someone is at fault for something that has gone wrong'.
11) **complex**
'complex' has the opposite meaning to 'simple' — 'complex' means 'difficult', whereas 'simple' means 'easy'.
12) **enemies**
'enemies' has the opposite meaning to 'friends' — 'enemies' are people you dislike, whereas 'friends' are people you like.
13) **fail**
'fail' has the opposite meaning to 'succeed' — 'fail' means 'to do badly', whereas 'succeed' means 'to do well'.
14) **disgusting**
'disgusting' has the opposite meaning to 'appealing' — 'disgusting' means 'unpleasant', whereas 'appealing' means 'really nice'.

Page 26 — Creative Writing

1) **many answers possible**
Some ideas are 'terrible', 'shocking' or 'awful'.
2) **many answers possible**
Some ideas are 'enormous', 'huge' or 'massive'.
3) **many answers possible**
Some ideas are 'freezing', 'icy' or 'frozen'.
4) **many answers possible**
Some ideas are 'lovely', 'beautiful' or 'wonderful'.
5) **many answers possible**
Some ideas are 'delighted', 'ecstatic' or 'overjoyed'.
6) **many answers possible**
Some ideas are 'ancient', 'aged' or 'elderly'.
7) **many answers possible**
Some ideas are 'delicious', 'amazing' or 'incredible'.
8) **many answers possible**
One idea is '"How long will you be in town?" asked Ariel.'
9) **many answers possible**
One idea is '"I'll be really well behaved if you bring me a present," pleaded Theo.'
10) **many answers possible**
One idea is '"Perhaps we could go down to the arcade together," suggested Amy.'
11) **many answers possible**
One idea is '"But I don't want to do my homework," whined Arthur.'
12) **many answers possible**
One idea is '" You can't do that!" Krys exclaimed.'
13) **many answers possible**
One idea is '"Smithson, bring me the map now," ordered the general.'
14) **many answers possible**
One idea is '"My leg is bleeding," cried the wounded policeman.'

Page 27 — Creative Writing

1) many answers possible
One idea is 'My town is quite small, but there are lots of nice shops, cafés and restaurants. There is always a busy market in the town square selling fresh fruit and vegetables.' You get one mark for each detailed sentence.

2) many answers possible
One idea is 'Yesterday the weather was really horrible because there were terrible storms. It was bitterly cold, very windy and rainy all day long.' You get one mark for each detailed sentence.

3) many answers possible
One idea is 'My school is a very old building covered in ivy plants on the outside. It has seventeen classrooms and a really big playground where we play at lunch time.' You get one mark for each detailed sentence.

4) many answers possible
One idea is 'For my birthday last year, my best friend came to my house and we opened my cards and presents while wearing coloured paper party hats. In the afternoon, more of my friends came round to my house for a super hero birthday cake and then we all went for a long walk in the woods.' You get one mark for each detailed sentence.

Page 28 — Non-Fiction Writing

1) P
This sentence is persuading the reader to watch Robo-cat — it has the instruction 'Watch Robo-cat'.

2) I
This sentence is informing the reader about Queen Elizabeth I — it tells the reader a fact about her reign.

3) I
This sentence is informing the reader about blue whales — it tells the reader a fact about their habitat and size.

4) P
This sentence is persuading the reader to try ballroom dancing — it has the instruction 'Try ballroom dancing'.

5) P
This sentence is persuading the reader to buy the new Flying Fox — it has the instruction 'buy the new Flying Fox'.

6) I
This sentence is informing the reader about the phone book in Iceland — it tells the reader how it is organised.

7) many answers possible
One idea is 'Please come to my birthday party because there will be the biggest bouncy castle in the world. We'll eat lots of delicious jelly and ice cream, and we'll play fun party games all afternoon.' There is one mark for each sentence that gives a reason why your friend should come to your party.

8) many answers possible
One idea is 'Come for a picnic on Sunday because the weather is supposed to be nice. We will have lots of tasty food.' There is one mark for each sentence that gives a reason why your friend should go for a picnic at the weekend.

Page 29 — Non-Fiction Writing

1) **Take three lemons and squeeze them. Stir sugar into the lemon juice. Pour fizzy water over the lemon and sugar. Mix the lemonade well. Pour it into a jug and add a slice of lemon to decorate it.**
You get one mark for each sentence you have correctly changed into an instruction (not including the sentence you were given).

2) **Walk to the bus stop. Wait for bus number 36. Get on the bus and ask for a single ticket to the library. Pay £1.70 and sit down on the bus. Press the button to let the bus driver know that you want to stop at the library.**
You get one mark for each sentence you have correctly changed into an instruction (not including the sentence you were given).

Pages 30-34 — Assessment Test 1

1) D
In the passage it says that "the Dinosaur Dipper roller coaster was the first thing Sanjay had seen".

2) E
In the passage when Sanjay asks if they can go on the Dinosaur Dipper, his dad says ""we're going to take Maya on some smaller rides first"."

3) E
In the passage it says "Sanjay saw an official-looking man helping people onto the ride."

4) C
In the passage it says that the teenagers "climb excitedly into the colourful carriages".

5) A
In the passage the ride is described as having "colourful" and "Brightly-painted" carriages.

6) C
In the passage it says that when Sanjay reached the front of the queue for the ride, he "wasn't sure that it looked fun after all".

7) B
In the passage it says that when Sanjay and his dad made their way toward the Dinosaur Dipper they "left Maya and Mum at the café".

8) B
'pulled' is closest in meaning to "tugged". Both words mean 'moved an object towards you'.

9) D
'talked' is closest in meaning to "chatted". Both words mean 'spoke'.

10) A
"swept" can mean 'pushed along forcefully', so A is correct because it describes how Sanjay was pushed quickly through the gate.

11) D
"echoed" and "begged" are verbs. They are both action words.

12) D
"huge" is the adjective. It describes the noun 'grin'.

13) C
'told' is correct — it means 'tell' in the past tense.

14) B
'couldn't' is correct — it means 'can not' in the past tense.

15) D
'had' is correct because it is in the past tense and completes the phrase 'had to stay in'.

16) C
'between' makes the most sense in this sentence and agrees with 'two trees' which follows.

17) A
'and' makes the most sense because it connects the two parts of the sentence.

18) C
'to' makes the most sense in this sentence.

19) A
'Finally' is correct because it is the last thing Jen and Malik did when they were building the den.

20) A
'sat' is correct — it means 'to sit' in the past tense.

Answers

21) E
The question mark at the end of the sentence is incorrect because the sentence is a statement, not a question.
22) A
There should be a set of inverted commas after 'shut up!' — inverted commas always come in pairs and go round the words that are spoken.
23) A
'would'nt' should be 'wouldn't'. This is a shortened version of 'would not' and the apostrophe replaces the missing letter 'o'.
24) D
The comma between 'with' and 'my' isn't needed.
25) B
'girl's' shouldn't have an apostrophe — the 's' at the end of 'girls' shows that it is a plural noun so it doesn't need an apostrophe.
26) C
'wallked' should be 'walked' — the root word is 'walk'.
27) C
'peace' should be 'piece'. These are homophones — 'piece' is correct because it means 'a portion of something', and peace means 'there is no war'.
28) D
'eassely' should be 'easily' — the root word is 'easy' which only has one 's'. The 'y' at the end of 'easy' changes to an 'i' when the suffix 'ly' is added.
29) E
'suny' should be 'sunny' — the correct spelling of the word has a double 'n'.
30) B
'wonderfull' should be 'wonderful' — the suffix 'ful' is spelt with a single 'l'.

Pages 35-39 — Assessment Test 2

1) C
In the passage it says that Anita goes into the garden "even though it was raining" and that "It was windy" when Anita took her first shot.
2) E
Anita had already seen part of the present because she had "peeled back a corner of the wrapping paper" on Aunt Angela's present and had a "quick peek".
3) A
In the passage it says that Anita "tore into the wrapping paper like a wild animal", which suggests that Anita ripped open the paper really quickly.
4) D
Anita tried to guess what her presents were when she had "just got home from school".
5) D
The passage refers to Poppy's "claws", which suggests that she is an animal, so she must be a pet.
6) B
In the passage it says that Anita used "one of Dad's garden gnomes and an upturned flowerpot" as a goal.
7) C
In the passage it says that Anita's first shot "missed the goal by a mile and ended up near the shed".
8) C
'torn' is closest in meaning to "ripped". Both words mean 'tear something up'.
9) E
'angry' is closest in meaning to "furious". Both words mean 'to be mad at something'.
10) D
'shocked' is closest in meaning to "surprised". Both words mean 'the feeling you get when you discover something unexpected'.

11) B
This is a simile because Anita is comparing herself to a wild animal by using the word "like".
12) C
"missed" is a verb because it is the 'action word' in this sentence.
13) A
'heard' should be 'herd'. These words are homophones — 'heard' is the past tense form of the verb 'to hear', and 'herd' refers to a group of animals, e.g. a herd of cows.
14) C
'babys' should be 'babies' — words ending in a consonant and a 'y' drop the 'y' and add 'ies' to make the plural.
15) B
'allmost' should be 'almost' — the correct prefix is 'al'.
16) C
'tastey' should be 'tasty' — the 'e' at the end of 'taste' is removed when 'y' is added to form 'tasty'.
17) D
'now' should be 'know' — 'know' has a silent 'k' at the beginning when it is the verb that means 'feel certain about something'.
18) C
'sissors' should be 'scissors' — there is a silent 'c'.
19) E
'terrable' should be 'terrible' — the correct suffix is 'ible'.
20) B
'adress' should be 'address' — it has a double 'd'.
21) A
'deer' is correct because it does not change in the plural.
22) D
'I' makes most sense because it shows who did the verb — 'noticed'.
23) D
'drinking' is the correct word here because it shows what the deer was doing.
24) E
'seen' is correct because it is in the past tense and completes the phrase 'it hadn't seen us'.
25) A
'after' makes most sense in this sentence.
26) C
The exclamation mark should be a question mark, because Robert is asking a question.
27) E
There should be a full stop at the end of the sentence.
28) A
The comma between 'known' and 'how' is unnecessary.
29) A
'Yvonnes' should be 'Yvonne's' — an apostrophe is needed here because the washing belongs to Yvonne.
30) B
'Castle' should be 'castle' — it doesn't need a capital letter because it's a common noun, not a proper noun.

Pages 40-44 — Assessment Test 3

1) D
In the passage Roger says "Robert Pershing Wadlow, the tallest man that ever lived, was nine years old. That's the same age as me!" This shows that Roger is nine years old.
2) A
In the passage it says that Robert Pershing Wadlow could carry his father up the stairs.
3) B
In the passage it says that Roger's dad gives Roger the new edition of the 'Book of World Records' every Christmas.

4) B
In the passage, it says that Roger's father "was a teacher".
5) E
In the passage Roger's father replies "wearily" with "'What now?'" and falls asleep — this suggests that he is uninterested in Roger's questions.
6) D
The 'World's best-selling book' is not mentioned in the passage.
7) C
At the end of the passage, Roger's father is snoring, which shows that he has fallen asleep.
8) A
'shouted' is closest in meaning to "yelled". Both words mean 'to call out loudly'.
9) D
'interesting' is closest in meaning to "fascinating". Both words mean 'something that grabs your attention'.
10) D
'grown' is closest in meaning to "sprouted". Both words mean 'to have produced something'.
11) D
"wounded" is the adjective — it describes the noun 'warthog'.
12) D
"Roger" and "Christmas" are both proper nouns because they are the name of a person and a festival.
13) B
'Them' should be 'them' — 'them' is not a proper noun, so it doesn't need a capital letter.
14) E
The question mark after "park" should be a full stop — the sentence is a statement, not a question.
15) D
There should be a comma between 'sugar' and 'eggs' to separate the items in a list.
16) E
The set of inverted commas after "him" aren't needed.
17) E
'oakthorpe' should be 'Oakthorpe' — it's a proper noun because it's the name of a place, so it should be capitalised.
18) B
'cant' should be 'can't' — this is a shortened version of 'cannot'. The apostrophe should be in the same place in the word as the missing letters.
19) E
The comma between 'to' and 'grow' is not needed.
20) E
There should be a set of inverted commas after 'Spain?' — inverted commas always come in pairs and go around the words that are spoken.
21) C
'exscuse' should be 'excuse' — there is no 's' right after the 'x'.
22) C
'destinasion' should be 'destination' — the correct suffix is 'tion'.
23) B
'accross' should be 'across' — there isn't a double 'c'.
24) D
'nun' should be 'none'. These words are homophones — a 'nun' is a member of a religious community, whereas 'none' means 'not any'.
25) C
'carm' should be 'calm' — the ending is 'lm'.
26) B
'an' is correct — there's only one elephant, and the word elephant begins with a vowel, so it must be 'an'.
27) B
'had' is correct because the person imagined the elephant in the past.
28) A
'by' is correct — it makes most sense in this sentence.
29) E
'began' is correct because the sentence is in the past tense.
30) D
'not' is correct because the zookeeper carries on laughing.

Pages 45-49 — Assessment Test 4

1) B
In the passage it says "A courtyard was built next to the motte, and this was known as the bailey."
2) C
In the passage it says that the palisade which surrounded the bailey was "an important part of the castle's defence".
3) A
The size of the castles is not given as a reason why the Normans built motte and bailey castles.
4) E
In the passage it says "There were many buildings within the bailey, including stables, storerooms, kitchens and living quarters." Schools are not mentioned in the passage.
5) D
In the passage, a motte is described as a "natural or man-made mound", a "high hill", part of a "motte and bailey castle" and made using "earth from the ditch". It is not described as a Roman fort.
6) D
In the passage it says "A wooden building called a 'keep' was built on top of the motte as a look-out point". A 'look-out' is a building used to watch for enemies.
7) D
In the passage it says that castles made of wood "caught fire easily" and that people started building stone castles because stone prevented them "from burning down".
8) D
'stop' is closest in meaning to "prevent". Both words mean 'to hold someone back'.
9) B
'attackers' is closest in meaning to "invaders". Both words mean 'a group who launch an assault'.
10) B
'round' is closest in meaning to "circular". Both words mean 'shaped like a circle'.
11) E
"easily" is an adverb because it describes the verb phrase "caught fire".
12) A
"deep" and "cheap" are adjectives — they both describe nouns.
13) B
'rushs' should be 'rushes' — the correct suffix is 'es'.
14) D
'hole' should be 'whole'. These words are homophones — 'hole' means 'an opening or gap in something' and 'whole' means 'all of something'.
15) A
'Their' should be 'There'. These words are homophones — 'their' means 'belonging to them', so 'there' is the word that makes the most sense in this sentence.
16) C
'seccond' should be 'second' — there is only one 'c' in the middle of the word.
17) B
'threw' should be 'through'. These words are homophones — 'threw' is the past tense of the verb 'to throw', but 'through' means 'to come out the other side of something'.

18) A
'whether' should be 'weather'. These words are homophones — 'weather' is correct because it means 'the climate conditions outside'.
19) B
'energetick' should be 'energetic' — there is no 'k' at the end of the word.
20) C
'bycycle' should be 'bicycle' — the correct prefix is 'bi'.
21) A
'do' should be 'Do' — it's the start of a sentence, so the word needs a capital letter.
22) A
'john' should be 'John' — it's a proper noun because it's the name of a person, so it needs a capital letter at the start of the word.
23) A
'theres' should be 'there's' — this is a shortened version of 'there is' and the apostrophe replaces the missing letter 'i'.
24) C
A question mark is needed after 'coat', because Ewa is asking a question.
25) D
A set of inverted commas is needed before 'Ready' to show that Georgina is speaking.
26) C
Mrs Rhency is asking for more than one grape, so the word that makes most sense is 'some'.
27) A
'behind' is the only word that makes sense in this sentence.
28) E
'was' makes the most sense in this sentence.
29) B
'bought' is correct — it is the past tense of the verb 'to buy', whereas 'brought' is the past tense of the verb 'to bring'.
30) D
'and' makes the most sense because it is a joining word which joins the two parts of the sentence.

Pages 50-54 — Assessment Test 5

1) A
In the poem it says "Little thing, in what dark den, / Lie you all the winter sleeping?".
2) E
In the poem it says "Keep away from corn".
3) C
In the poem the field mouse is referred to as a "Pretty, quiet harmless thing" — "harmless" is another word for gentle.
4) B
In the poem it says "you must not steal the grain / He [the farmer] has stacked with so much pain." In this line, "so much pain" means 'with so much care'.
5) C
In the poem it says "Make your hole where mosses spring, / Underneath the tall oak's shadow".
6) D
The field mouse finds food, eats, plays and makes a nest, but there is no mention of it going to the farmer's house.
7) A
"scarcely" means 'hardly'. In the next verse of the poem the field mouse is referred to as "Little thing", suggesting it is small, so it hardly causes the grass to move as it passes.

8) A
'chewing' is closest in meaning to "nibbling" — both words mean 'eating little bits'.
9) E
'heaps' is closest in meaning to "stacks". Both words mean 'piles up'.
10) C
'drops' is closest in meaning to "sheds". Both words mean 'loses something'.
11) D
"soft" and "merry" are adjectives. They both describe nouns.
12) A
"Find" is the verb. It's an action word.
13) A
'going' makes the most sense in this sentence because it's describing what they are planning to do in the future.
14) C
'because' is correct — it introduces the second part of the sentence.
15) D
'wear' makes most sense in this sentence because the writer is describing what people will be wearing at the party.
16) C
'am' is correct because it completes the phrase 'I am going'.
17) B
'too' is correct — it means 'as well'.
18) D
'who' is correct as the writer is discussing which people they are going to invite to their party.
19) C
'but' is correct because it is a conjunction which introduces the second part of the sentence.
20) E
'said' is correct because it completes the phrase 'have said'.
21) B
A comma is needed between 'hedgehogs' and 'owls' — items in a list are separated using commas.
22) D
A question mark is needed after 'swim' because Liam is asking a question.
23) D
A set of inverted commas is needed after 'sale' — inverted commas always come in pairs around the words that are spoken.
24) B
'mr' should be 'Mr' — the word needs a capital letter because it's part of a proper noun.
25) A
'its' should be 'it's' — this is a shortened version of 'it is' and the apostrophe replaces the missing letter 'i'.
26) D
'untill' should be 'until' — it is spelt with a single 'l'.
27) D
'woble' should be 'wobble' — there is a double 'b' in the middle of the word.
28) E
'loose' should be 'lose' — 'loose' means 'unsecured' and 'lose' means 'to not know where something is'.
29) A
'puppys' should be 'puppies' — words ending in a consonant and a 'y' drop the 'y' and add 'ies' to make the plural.
30) C
'stares' should be 'stairs'. These words are homophones — 'stares' means 'glares at something' and 'stairs' are a series of steps.

Pages 55-59 — Assessment Test 6

1) D
In the passage it says that Aunt Florence "dyed her long hair".
2) A
In the passage it says that Aunt Florence gave Ruby the key on the "day before yesterday", which means 'two days ago'.
3) C
Aunt Florence whispered when she told Ruby about the key, so she was talking quietly.
4) E
Aunt Florence went through the door when she was Ruby's age.
5) D
In the passage it says that the door is in "the attic of Grandpa's old house", so it is not in Aunt Florence's home.
6) C
Aunt Florence says to Ruby that the door will only reveal itself "if the person holding the key believes that the magical door exists".
7) E
Ruby was surprised because a "wonky, wooden door slowly appeared in the wall".
8) D
'invented' is closest in meaning to "imaginary". Both words mean 'made up'.
9) C
'show' is closest in meaning to "reveal". Both words mean 'display something so it can be seen'.
10) A
'ordinary' is closest in meaning to "unimpressive". Both words mean 'normal'.
11) C
"quietly" is an adverb because it describes the verb "said".
12) B
This is an example of alliteration. Alliteration is when a sound is repeated at the beginning of words in a phrase — the 'd' sound is repeated here.
13) B
'group's' should be 'groups' — 'groups' is a plural word and doesn't show possession so it doesn't need an apostrophe.
14) E
'Birthday' doesn't need a capital letter because it is in the middle of a sentence and it isn't a proper noun.
15) E
There should be an exclamation mark or a full stop rather than a question mark at the end of the sentence — the sentence is not a question.
16) D
There shouldn't be a comma between 'activities' and 'and' because it is at the end of the list.
17) E
This is a question so it should end with a question mark rather than an exclamation mark.
18) A
'Freds' should be 'Fred's' — the apostrophe shows that the job belongs to Fred.
19) B
There should be a second set of inverted commas after 'help!' to show the end of the speech.
20) A
'Its' should be 'It's' — it is the contracted form of 'It is', so it needs to have an apostrophe.
21) B
'copys' should be 'copies' — when a word ends in a consonant and then a 'y' you drop the 'y' and add 'ies' to make the plural.
22) A
'spesial' should be 'special' — it has a 'c' rather than an 's'.
23) A
'peared' should be 'peered' — the root word is 'peer'.
24) B
'gitar' should be 'guitar' — it has a silent 'u' in the middle.
25) E
'tide' should be 'tied'. These words are homophones — the 'tide' is 'the rise and fall of water' whereas 'tied' is the past tense form of the verb 'to tie'.
26) E
'wasn't' is correct — it is the shortened form of 'was not'.
27) B
'when' is correct — it completes the phrase 'when I got there'.
28) C
'looked' is correct — it is the past tense form of the verb 'to look'.
29) A
'had' is correct — it is the past tense form of the verb 'to have'.
30) D
'told' is correct — it is the past tense form of the verb 'to tell'.

Pages 60-64 — Assessment Test 7

1) B
In the passage it says that the Ancient Olympic Games "took place in a stadium in the valley of Olympia".
2) C
In the passage it says that "The Olympic Games were held for over a thousand years until they were banned" — 'thousand' is the written word for the number 1000.
3) E
In the passage it says that the winners were "presented with a special crown made from olive leaves".
4) B
In the passage it says that "The games started with worship" in honour of Zeus.
5) E
In the passage it says that the hoplite race was "challenging" because "the runners had to wear armour".
6) D
In the passage it says that the Olympic Games were "held to honour Zeus, king of the gods" — there is no mention of a king of the Greeks.
7) C
In the passage it says that the statue of Zeus was "made from gold and ivory" and that it was "six times bigger" than a person. This means that the statue would have looked very impressive.
8) E
"to honour Zeus" is closest in meaning to 'to praise Zeus' — both mean 'to show your admiration'.
9) A
"competitors" is closest in meaning to 'contestants'. Both words mean 'the people that take part in a challenge'.
10) A
"strength" is closest in meaning to 'power'. Both words mean 'being strong'.
11) D
"great" and "special" are adjectives because they both describe nouns.
12) C
"include" is a verb because it is an action word.
13) A
'Dangerus' should be 'Dangerous' — the suffix 'ous' has been added to the root word 'danger'.
14) B
'tuff' should be 'tough' — the ending is 'ough'.

Answers

15) A
'monkies' should be 'monkeys' — words ending in a vowel and a 'y' add 's' to make the plural.
16) A
'Jokeingly' should be 'Jokingly' — you need to remove the 'e' before adding the suffix 'ing', then you can add the suffix 'ly' to 'joking'.
17) B
'toucht' should be 'touched' — the suffix 'ed' is added to the root word 'touch'.
18) C
'throne' should be 'thrown'. These words are homophones — 'throne' means 'a special chair where a royal person sits', whereas 'thrown' is the past tense form of the verb 'to throw'.
19) B
'memerable' should be 'memorable' — the vowel should be 'o', not 'e'.
20) B
'knifes' should be 'knives' — the 'fe' in 'knife' changes to 'ves' to make the plural.
21) A
'some' is correct because it makes the most sense in this sentence.
22) E
'won' is correct because it is the correct past tense form of the verb 'to win'.
23) A
'made' is the correct word because it is the past tense form of the verb 'to make'.
24) D
'had' is the correct word because it is in the past tense and completes the phrase 'had lost'.
25) B
'will' is correct because it is about the future and completes the phrase, 'there will be'.
26) D
'hadnt' should be 'hadn't' — there should be an apostrophe between the 'n' and the 't' to replace the missing 'o'.
27) E
The inverted commas at the end of the sentence aren't needed because the sentence doesn't include any speech.
28) D
The apostrophe at the end of 'books' isn't needed because 'books' is a plural rather than a possessive.
29) B
'Trees' should be 'trees' — 'trees' doesn't need a capital letter because the word is not a proper noun or at the start of a sentence.
30) C
There should be a comma between 'teacups' and 'the' to separate two items in a list.

Pages 65-69 — Assessment Test 8

1) E
In the poem the child describes the "wintry sun", "jolly fire", "cold candle" and the stars in the sky, but doesn't mention the moon.
2) C
In the poem the child says "my nurse doth wrap / Me in my comforter and cap" — this means the nurse helps the child to dress.
3) C
In the poem the child says "At morning in the dark I rise". It's dark when the child gets up so he needs to light a candle.
4) D
In the poem the child says that "The cold wind burns my face, and blows / Its frosty pepper up my nose." This means that the wind is so cold that it's stinging the child's face.

5) A
In the poem the child goes outside last.
6) C
The first verse is about the way the sun rises late and then sets after a few hours.
7) E
In the poem the child says "Black are my steps on silver sod" — this means his footsteps have melted the frost.
8) A
'Trembling' is closest in meaning to "shivering". Both words mean 'shaking'.
9) A
'Merry' is closest in meaning to "jolly". Both words mean 'happy'.
10) B
'Travel around' is closest in meaning to "explore". They both mean 'visit new places'.
11) C
"frozen" is the adjective — it describes the noun "bones".
12) B
It is an example of a simile because a simile describes something as being like something else. In the poem, the hill and lake are described as being covered in frost like the icing on a "wedding-cake".
13) C
There should be a comma between 'Sven' and 'Paula' because commas separate items in a list.
14) E
'france' should be 'France' — it's a proper noun so it should be capitalised.
15) B
The comma between 'determined' and 'to' isn't needed.
16) A
There should be a comma between 'tiger' and 'which' to separate the parts of the sentence.
17) D
There shouldn't be a comma between 'thick' and 'mud' — 'thick' is not a separate item in the list.
18) C
There should be inverted commas between 'crowd' and 'Give' — inverted commas always come in pairs around the words that are spoken.
19) C
'theyre' should be 'they're' — there should be an apostrophe between 'y' and 'r' to replace the missing 'a'.
20) E
The exclamation mark should be between 'scary' and the inverted commas.
21) E
'awfull' should be 'awful' — there is only one 'l' at the end.
22) B
'pityful' should be 'pitiful' — the 'y' in 'pity' is changed to an 'i' when the suffix 'ful' is added.
23) E
'brake' should be 'break'. These words are homophones — 'brake' means 'to slow down a vehicle' whereas 'break' means 'to damage something'.
24) D
'populer' should be 'popular' — the correct vowel is 'a' rather than 'e'.
25) C
'draging' should be 'dragging' — an extra 'g' is added to 'drag' when the suffix 'ing' is added.
26) E
'of' is correct because it makes the most sense in this sentence.

27) A
'bought' is correct because it is the correct past tense form of the verb 'to buy'.
28) B
'beside' is correct because it makes the most sense in this sentence.
29) D
'couldn't' is correct because it means 'wasn't able to' in the past tense.
30) C
'ride' is correct because it is in the present tense and completes the phrase 'I can ride'.

Progress Chart

Use this chart to keep track of your scores for the Assessment Tests.

You can do each test more than once — download extra answer sheets from cgpbooks.co.uk/11plus/answer-sheets or scan the QR code on the right.

Answer Sheets

	First Go	**Second Go**	**Third Go**
Test 1	Date: Score:	Date: Score:	Date: Score:
Test 2	Date: Score:	Date: Score:	Date: Score:
Test 3	Date: Score:	Date: Score:	Date: Score:
Test 4	Date: Score:	Date: Score:	Date: Score:
Test 5	Date: Score:	Date: Score:	Date: Score:
Test 6	Date: Score:	Date: Score:	Date: Score:
Test 7	Date: Score:	Date: Score:	Date: Score:
Test 8	Date: Score:	Date: Score:	Date: Score:

Look back at your scores once you've done all the Assessment Tests. Each test is out of 30 marks.

Work out which kind of mark you scored most often:

0-17 marks — Go back to basics and work on your question technique.

18-25 marks — You're nearly there — go back over the questions you found tricky.

26-30 marks — You're an English whizz. Go on to Practice Book Age 9-10.